LET'S
MAKE
SUSHI!

LET'S MAKE SUSHI!

Step-by-Step Tutorials and Essential Recipes for Rolls, Nigiri, Sashimi and More from a Master Sushi Chef

CHEF ANDY MATSUDA

Founder of The Sushi Chef Institute

PAGE STREET
PUBLISHING CO.

PAGE STREET
PUBLISHING CO.

First published in 2023 by
Page Street Publishing Co.
27 Congress Street, Suite 1511
Salem, MA 01970
www.pagestreetpublishing.com

Distributed by Macmillan, sales in Canada by The Canadian Manda Group.

26   25   24   23   22   1   2   3   4   5

ISBN-13: 978-1-64567-708-6
ISBN-10: 1-64567-708-7

Library of Congress Control Number: 2022942786

Cover and book design by Meg Baskis for Page Street Publishing Co.
Photography by Joshua Fontal

Printed and bound in China by 1010 Printing International Limited

I WOULD LIKE TO DEDICATE THIS BOOK TO AND THANK MY FATHER,
HIROICHI MATSUDA, AND MY MOTHER, MAKIKO,
WHO WERE THE STARTING POINT OF MY SUSHI LIFE.

I AM GRATEFUL THAT I HAD THE OPPORTUNITY TO GROW UP AS A CHEF
FROM MY EARLY CHILDHOOD, HAD GREAT EXPECTATIONS AND
THAT MY PARENTS GAVE ME FREEDOM TO EXPERIENCE THINGS.

ALSO, I AM GRATEFUL FOR MY FAMILY, MY WIFE, SETSU,
AND MY DAUGHTER, AIKA, WHO HAVE SUPPORTED ME IN MY AMERICAN
NANAKOROBIYAOKI NO SEIKATSU (LIFE OF SEVEN FALLS AND EIGHT RISES).

CONTENTS

FOREWORD

Sushi is one of the toughest Asian cuisines to learn because it has almost no relation to other foods most folks make. A lot of other cuisines can be guessed at or contextualized. Stir fry is just sauté with a few new ingredients. Salads are vegetable medleys with a dressing for the most part, and even the dressings are a combination of an oil, an acid then some flavorings and seasonings. Cooks can usually use the rules in their repertoire to extrapolate a dish, even if it is foreign; there are some small parts to latch onto that are somewhat familiar. But not for sushi. Sushi is a delicious, strange new world that has no road maps cooks can identify or start to make sense of. So, writing a cookbook on sushi is even tougher than most subjects. Luckily, you are in the hands of a great chef and guide in these pages.

I've known Chef Andy for over 20 years. When I was in my twenties, I had a firm grasp on cooking Thai and Chinese cuisines from growing up in those cultures. I had more than my 10,000 hours thanks to my family's three generations of restaurant, shopkeeping and farming experience. But I was always fascinated by sushi and Japanese cuisine. Through the context I had with my Chinese, Thai and French cooking background, I did my best to figure out how to make my favorite sushi and sashimi dishes for years. But even with my extensive experience, I was only guessing. It really took expert guidance and training from Chef Andy to give me the deep, knowledgeable push that opened up the world of sushi to me and really shaped my career.

I trained under Chef Andy for a time and learned the building blocks of making sushi. He taught me the fundamentals of making sushi rice and sushi vinegar, and how critical it was for both to be prepared perfectly. Then we moved on to fish selection and preparation, and continued on to mastering the dressing, sauces and finally, the plated sushi and sashimi. Chef Andy always patiently shared his secrets and wove in the history and stories behind this cuisine into my lessons, which caused me to foster a deeper and more meaningful connection to this traditional food. This is what this book will do for you. It will teach and guide you through into this new, fascinating world and hopefully change you forever.

Happy Cooking!

—JET TILA

INTRODUCTION

Hello! My name is Andy Matsuda. After working as a sushi chef for many years, I decided to open the Sushi Chef Institute 20 years ago with the hopes of bringing professional chefs, and anybody who wanted to learn about it, closer to Japanese cuisine. I am excited to now share some of my knowledge in this book. The following pages describe the basic techniques and preparations for making traditional sushi in Japanese food culture. It is said that the sushi boom began in America about 50 years ago; since then, it's become a nonstop industry that continues to grow. In 1981, when I came to the United States, I could see the sushi boom very much alive among the people eating in Santa Monica sushi bars and not only in Little Tokyo, but in downtown Los Angeles where it all started. This phenomenon continued to expand even more across the West Coast after the 1984 Los Angeles Olympics, and Japanese food culture started to prosper all over the world.

In the Western food scene, instead of Japanese *edomae* sushi, which is mostly simple sushi rolls, and *hako zushi* (pressed sushi), which uses fresh, raw and sometimes cooked or cured fish and seafood, special locally inspired rolls, such as California Rolls (page 61), Spicy Tuna Rolls (page 62) or Philadeliphia Rolls (page 76), became a major trend and opened the doors even more for Japanese cuisine in Western culture. Now, we are entering an era in which people from different cultural backgrounds have incorporated sushi into their diet often, from once or twice a month to every week! In that sense, I was inspired by the sushi

roll culture, which sparked the sushi boom here in the United States, to share my knowledge in this book so that as many people as possible can feel closer to the Japanese cuisine they love.

This book will teach you to easily make sushi at home. It is for those who have never made or eaten homemade sushi. My goal is to share with you an attainable and simple way to bring sushi to your table. I'll share my simple techniques for making sushi rolls, *nigiri* and *sashimi*. Hopefully, you'll be able to incorporate new healthy meals into your diet and enjoy a fun activity that you can share with your family and friends, that brings you closer to each other in the process. My hope is that, with this book, children who have grown up with Japanese anime and manga will become closer to Japanese food culture, and maybe become their own artistic sushi chef.

With this book, I aim to expand your knowledge of sushi and the many forms it takes today, from raw fish to cooked fish and vegetables. I'll show you how sushi can become a part of your healthy diet. There are endless possibilities with this cuisine. I will take you step by step through my techniques so you can bring this piece of Japanese culture into your home. If some of the ingredients are not available in your area, you can always create your own sushi rolls with the products your local market has to offer.

Yarimashoo! (Let's get to it!)

THE ESSENTIAL TOOLS & INGREDIENTS

Before going into more detail about the modern tools you will be using, I want to share a story. My first sushi tool was a *yanagi* knife. It was a gift from my master, and I still have it. In the beginning, I had no idea how to maintain the knife and I messed up a few times. But I didn't give up and kept sharpening the knife for a long time. I have many fond memories with my first knife. It was the only knife I brought with me to the United States in 1981; we became immigrants together. I hope you can make beautiful memories with your sushi tools, too!

Now, let's first get familiar with the history and cultural significance behind the most important tools in sushi making. Many of the first Japanese tools used for sushi are known to have been created back in the middle of the Edo period in the years 1603–1867. Edo, known as Tokyo in modern times, became the capital of Japan. Many people started coming to Edo, the food industry bloomed and cooking became a very important profession. In old Japan, we used to have many sword makers. They used to make samurai's swords, known as *katana*. Usually, samurai would carry a big and a small katana, but after samurai started to disappear, sword makers lost their business. From that moment, chefs started to use small katanas as cooking tools. Eventually, special small cooking swords were made, and those cooking swords evolved into our modern knives. Origin-ally, sword makers created Japanese knives and swords from the same materials. However, with the arrival of the popular Western knife in the early 1900s, the usage of other metals, such as stainless steel, began.

People used to cook in stoves, called *kamado*, made from bricks and stones, and eventually ceramic. Rice was made in a big steel pot that had a wooden lid. Cooks would measure ingredients with a square wooden cup called a *masu*, which is very similar to the one that is brought to you when drinking sake at restaurants. Japan's masu cup holds 6 ounces (175 ml), whereas an American cup holds 8 ounces (240 ml). Most tools in Japan used to be made of wood or bamboo. Now, due to health regulations, most are made of plastic; however, wooden tools are still available and used by many people.

As far as the common ingredients for sushi go, since weather, resources and culture are different throughout Japan, each region produces its own signature ingredients, which eventually would become popular regional food. This is something that is still true today. In Japanese culture, people rely on the ingredients that are in season and available at their local markets. There are unique vegetables and seafood everywhere. That is why I recommend you check your local markets and try using local products!

ESSENTIAL SUSHI-MAKING TOOLS

Professional sushi chefs have an array of tools at their disposal. To truly become a master, you need to work with all of them. However, you can still make expert-level sushi with just a few basics. Here is what you need:

VERY SHARP KNIFE: This can be any Western-style multi-purpose knife. The most popular size for this knife is 8 to 10 inches (20 to 25 cm).

MAKISU: *Makisu* is the bamboo mat used for making sushi rolls. It was first made in Japan more than 200 years ago. Recently, sushi chefs like to cover the makisu with plastic wrap so rice doesn't stick to it. This is particularly helpful with Uramaki (Rice-Outside Rolls; page 57), such as the California Roll (page 61). The U.S. health department also recommends wrapping your mat in plastic wrap. Some sushi mats are made of silicone, but I prefer the traditional bamboo mat. These can be found in most Asian markets in their kitchen tool corner. It is usually not expensive.

RICE COOKER: In Japan, most households have a rice cooker. Japanese families eat steamed rice every day, about three times a day. For us, a rice cooker is a daily-use appliance. Most home rice cookers have about a 10-cup (2-kg) capacity. The most popular rice cooker brands in Japan are Tiger® and Zojirushi®. Although rice cookers are preferred, I'll also show you how to cook sushi rice in a regular pot (see page 19).

HANGIRI: When making Sushi Rice (page 19), Japanese families use a wooden tub called a *hangiri* for mixing the rice with the vinegar. This wooden tub is used to more easily control the temperature, but if you don't have one, you can use a plastic bowl instead. Stainless-steel bowls lose heat faster than wooden containers. Keeping the sushi rice hot helps the *sushi-zu* (sushi vinegar) penetrate deep into the rice and flavor it. If the rice temperature lowers too quickly, the sushi-zu won't flavor the rice deeply. In the United States, however, due to health regulations, you are not allowed to use a traditional wooden hangiri in a professional kitchen.

RICE PADDLE: This paddle can be made of plastic or wood. It is used for mixing the steamed rice and the sushi-zu. The paddle helps break up the rice and avoid big balls of rice from forming when mixing in the sushi-zu.

PLASTIC WRAP: Plastic wrap is regularly used in roll making so the rolls look cleaner. It helps prevent the rolls from falling apart when cutting them. Plastic wrap is also used to safely store fish and vegetables and keep them from drying out.

EXTRA TOOLS A PROFESSIONAL SUSHI CHEF USES

If you want to take your sushi making to the next level, here is a bit more info on tools used by masters from Japan and all over the world.

YANAGI KNIFE: A *yanagi* knife is a skinny, long knife mostly used to slice fish for nigiri, sushi rolls or sashimi.

DEBA KNIFE: A *deba* knife is wider at the bottom and narrows a bit toward the tip. It is a little shorter than the yanagi. This is used mostly for fileting fish.

USUBA KNIFE: The *usuba* knife has a wide blade that doesn't narrow toward the tip. This knife is used mostly for vegetable cutting, and is especially utilized by chefs when cutting daikon and other vegetable garnishes for plating.

GYUTO KNIFE: The *gyuto* knife is the equivalent of a Western chef's knife. It has many different purposes, such as cutting meat and vegetables. The most popular length for this knife is 8 to 10 inches (20 to 25 cm).

MORIBASHI: These are chopsticks used for handling small ingredients or fish when plating. They are made of stainless steel and the grip is wooden. The ends are very thin and come to a sharp point. The reason *moribashi* are made of stainless steel is that, when used for plating sashimi dishes, the stainless steel prevents the transfer of body heat to the fish; in addition, they are easier to keep clean.

SERVING PLATES: In Japan, depending on the season, we use different plate colors. In spring, we can use light blue or green plates. For summer, glass plates. For fall and winter, we commonly use black or dark plates. Depending on what you are making (sushi rolls, sashimi or nigiri) the shape of the plate is also important. You can play with round, square, deep and flat plates until you find the perfect match for your dish.

WASHING BOWL AND BASKET: When washing rice, you'll need the right bowl and basket size. Find the ones that fit the amount of rice that you are preparing. The process is easier and less messy if you have these two when rinsing and drying rice. Stainless-steel bowls and a fine-mesh strainer work just fine for this process.

CHEF ANDY'S NOTE ON KNIVES: It's important to point out that Japanese knives are made of carbon steel and white steel, whereas Western knives are mostly made of stainless steel. This means Japanese knives are more susceptible to rusting. Although Japanese knives can be sharper than Western knives, they require much more maintenance. Western knives, also known as chef's knives or home knives, are much easier to maintain. Japanese knife blades are one-sided, and that's another characteristic that makes them sharper than Western knives.

IMPORTANT INGREDIENTS

JAPONICA RICE: Look for short grain or medium-short grain. Oddly enough, japonica rice is mostly grown and milled in Sacramento, California, home to many types of rice. This area has been developing its rice-growing for over 150 years and even exports rice to Japan and other Asian countries.

Try your best to find japonica short-grain rice, which is what most sushi masters like to use, since its quality is higher, the moisture and stickiness are more balanced and you will end up with better sushi rice. If you are not able to find it, you can use short- or medium-grain rice that is not Japanese, but be aware that it might be drier and a little stickier. Jasmine or long-grain rice will not work well when making sushi rice since these varieties don't have the stickiness and sweetness that characterize Japanese rice. You can buy short-grain sushi rice online, in most Asian super-markets or at regular supermarkets in the Asian foods section. Rice from Japan tends to be more expensive, but it is very tasty and higher quality. If you can find Japanese rice, buy that.

CHEF ANDY'S NOTE ON RICE: In November, you may see a sticker on rice's packaging that says *shinmai*, or "new crop." Rice is harvested in late October or early November in Sacramento. Newly harvested rice retains its moisture from the harvest for about four months and thus requires less water when cooking. By the end of March, rice is considered "old crop." New-crop rice requires a bit less water for cooking and is good for steaming, whereas old-crop rice is good for sushi rice. Old-crop rice has about 12 percent moisture, which helps the sushi-zu penetrate the grain better, making it more flavorful. For regular steamed rice, new crop is better.

NORI: Nori is dried seaweed processed into sheets for sushi rolls. It has been made into sheets in Japan for about 250 years. It is cut along the multiple parallel lines that can be seen in the sheet.

These days, seaweed comes mainly from China. Many years ago, Japanese nori companies looked for a new location to develop seaweed farming. They found the China Sea to have good conditions. In Japan, nori companies have to follow many rules and regulations to release the final products to the market. In China, the regulations to ship to other countries are not as strict. Sushi nori should be nice and crispy, not too thick and not too thin. Your nori sheets should be about 7½ x 8 inches (19 x 20 cm). Black nori is untoasted; for sushi, you want to use the toasted kind that has a nice green tone. Japanese nori for sushi is not seasoned. Seasoned nori is mostly for snacking.

SESAME SEEDS: Mainly used in roll making, sesame seeds must not be raw, but the roasted variety, to add a nice flavor to the rolls.

WASABI: Wasabi root, which is in the mustard family and tastes similar to horseradish, is very expensive and hard to grow. The most commonly used form of wasabi is the powdered version. Wasabi root is not as spicy and has a sweeter side to it. Powdered wasabi has a stronger kick to it and holds its flavor longer than the root. The powdered version is what is used at most sushi bars. If you have the opportunity to try wasabi paste, I definitely recommend you do so, but using powdered wasabi is totally fine. Sushi chefs add wasabi between the fish and sushi rice when making nigiri. When eating sashimi, wasabi is mixed with soy sauce. Wasabi also has many antibacterial properties.

GARI (SLICED PICKLED GINGER): *Gari* is widely used at sushi bars and eaten with nigiri or sushi rolls. It is used to cleanse your palate between bites. Just like wasabi, gari has antibacterial properties. Pickled ginger used to be made by sushi chefs at home. Nowadays, it is mostly factory made. When fresh ginger comes from Asia, it is peeled, sliced and parboiled. Then, it is marinated in sweet vinegar. Gari can be stored for many days due to its pickled nature. You can find premade gari at any store with a good Asian foods section. The best gari is made with natural sugar, but it might be a challenge to find it.

SHOYU (SOY SAUCE): Soy sauce is made from fermented wheat, soybeans, salt and water. The most popular soy sauce is dark soy with 14 percent sodium. In Japan, we have different types of soy sauce: light soy sauce, tamari soy sauce and white soy sauce. We use all of these for different kinds of dishes, since each one enhances the dishes differently. For sushi, we use dark soy. It is more flavorful and affordable and you can find it in most grocery stores. Nowadays, companies have plenty of gluten-free options.

RICE VINEGAR: Sake is made from rice; the sake lees, or the by-product of the rice plant after making sake, are used to create rice vinegar. It is an integral part of sushi making, flavoring the rice and acting as a preservative; it has antibacterial properties.

NITSUME (SUSHI SAUCE): *Nitsume* is usually called eel sauce. I like to make my own eel sauce from real eel, but you can find it in many stores. These ones are mostly made with sugar and soy sauce. If you would like to enjoy a more traditional sushi sauce, I would recommend looking for sauces made with real eel, but these might be difficult to find. The sushi sauces that you can find in supermarkets all have different flavors since their ingredients are different; try different brands and see which one is most pleasant to your palate.

OTHER POPULAR JAPANESE INGREDIENTS USED IN SUSHI MAKING

MIRIN: This ingredient is sweet rice wine (sake). The process for making mirin is the same as for sake, but mirin has a much sweeter taste. This is one of the main ingredients used in Japanese cuisine. It is particularly important to add sweetness to simmering dishes.

COOKING SAKE: Known as jozo (brewer's) sake, it is the sake with the easiest and lowest cost of production, made from steamed rice, fermented rice and alcohol. It is a very important foundation for Japanese cuisine.

MAME NORI (SOY PAPER): *Mame* nori is made from soybeans. It is softer than seaweed nori and easier to cut and manipulate. It comes in a variety of colors and is ideal for people who don't like seaweed.

KONBU: This kind of long seaweed, a giant kelp, is found in the oceans in the north of Japan. It is dried at the beach, and it is used for making Dashi (page 32).

TAMARI: Tamari is a much thicker soy sauce. It is used for making Ponzu (page 160), teriyaki sauce and sushi sauce.

FURIKAKE: This product is very popular in Japan to use as a topping for steamed rice. Easy to use, *furikake* adds tasty flavors to rice, without any other pairings for your rice. It is a blend of many types of dried ingredients, such as seaweed, black or white sesame seeds, egg and fish flakes, such as salmon. All furikake is made of dried products and has a long and stable shelf life.

BONITO FLAKES: These are made by cooking and smoking skipjack filet, then drying and shaving it. I really enjoy how these are made and it's very interesting when you can shave the hard filets yourself and have very fresh bonito flakes. I think it has a nice umami taste. These are used in Japanese cuisine when making *ichiban dashi* (primary dashi), the foundation of many Japanese soups and sauces.

TOBIKO (FLYING FISH EGGS): These have a wide color selection: orange, red, black, green and yellow. *Tobiko* are used for contrast and decoration on top of sushi rolls. You should be able to find tobiko mostly at Asian supermarkets or online. The colors don't play a big role in their flavor. They tend to be very similar in taste.

YAMAGOBO (PICKLED BURDOCK ROOT): Japanese people eat many pickled vegetables. It is a big part of our culture and *yamagobo* is no exception. It can be used as a garnish or to put inside sushi rolls and more.

KAIWARE (DAIKON SPROUTS): These are used widely for sashimi garnishing or inside hand rolls and sushi rolls. This microgreen can be also used in salads and other dishes. It's known to be very healthy. The flavor of *kaiware* can be considered grassy and semisweet combined with a little peppery note.

QUAIL EGGS: Popular in oyster shooters and as a topping with *uni* (sea urchin). Quail eggs are very similar in taste to chicken eggs. Since they are smaller, it makes them great for plating. It is usually safe to eat raw quail eggs, but if you are pregnant or have a compromised immune system, I would advise you not to consume them. I recommend rinsing them in cold water before using them to clean their surface.

SHISO; A.K.A. OOBA OR PERILLA: This Japanese herb is a member of the mint family. Strong and flavorful, it is used mainly for sashimi garnishing, tempura and more traditional sushi styles. You can find this herb mostly at Asian supermarkets. If you can't find shiso leaves, you can substitute a cucumber fan when garnishing sashimi.

ESSENTIAL PREP

My students usually ask me how long it takes to learn the skills to make good sushi. I like to say that in just two years, you can build the confidence. This is not only true for professionals, but for anybody who has a passion for sushi making.

One of the things that took me the longest to understand was the perfect cooking conditions for Sushi Rice (page 19). Sushi rice is very important because it acts as the foundation for your sushi. It also is an important complement in terms of flavor and texture. When I host one-day workshops at the Sushi Chef Institute for nonprofessional cooks, dealing with the sushi rice is the hardest part for them. My professional students also struggle in the beginning, but after they learn the tricks and techniques, it becomes easier. In this chapter, we'll go over making perfect sushi rice.

We will also begin to get familiar with sourcing and prepping your fish and seafood. I will go over what to look for when buying fresh fish, and show you my preparation techniques for seafood, so you can have everything ready to go to start making rolls, nigiri and sashimi.

My first contact with fish was at a young age at my father's restaurant. I loved, and still do, handling fish and seafood. Working with fish at my father's restaurant was an advantage for me; by the time I started working at other restaurants, I was very used to working with fish. When I began my first job in Osaka as a starting sushi chef at a high-volume takeout shop, I practiced my cutting skills with *saba* (mackerel), an inexpensive fish that Japanese people love to eat. There, my *senpai* (an elder or more experienced mentor) taught me more about how to handle fish and seafood. Fish comes in so many shapes: big, small, flat, fat, long and skinny, all very different. Same goes with other seafood, such as clams, shellfish, sea urchin, octopus, squid and others. You must understand their anatomy so you can cut them correctly. For me, one of the biggest challenges as a sushi chef was prepping and cutting fish and seafood, but at the same time it was always fun learning the skills.

In this chapter, I want to share with you the fundamental skills for sushi making. There are not many sushi schools around the world and people may try to learn on the job, but restaurants are extremely fast-paced environments, which doesn't make them the best place for learning. Chefs are usually very busy, and they might not want to let you play with expensive fish. Most Japanese chefs say that you should learn by eye; it's rare that they take time to teach you step by step. In this chapter and throughout this book, I want to teach you the fundamental techniques step by step so you can practice every day. My hope is that you will even be able to teach someone in the future and continue to share Japanese food culture.

MASTERING SUSHI RICE

HOW TO MAKE SUSHI-ZU
(SUSHI VINEGAR)

MAKES 3 CUPS (720 ML) IF INGREDIENTS ARE
MEASURED IN STANDARD U.S. CUPS

Sushi-zu is a well-guarded secret. Each chef has their own recipe for making the seasoned vinegar. It is paramount for making sushi rice, which further illustrates the importance of rice when making sushi. Sushi-zu tends to be tangy and strong in taste on its own. Its saltiness, sourness and sweetness are balanced when konbu is added to it. Konbu is an important part of this recipe as it creates a balanced flavor. Sushi-zu should be aged for at least two weeks prior to using, which allows the konbu to mellow and add umami to the vinegar. You can buy konbu at most Asian supermarkets or online. If you cannot find konbu, be aware that your sushi-zu will have a strong, punchy vinegar taste to it.

Many Japanese recipes are given in ratios, or parts, rather than exact measurements. A primary example of this is the recipe for sushi-zu. What is a "part"? It could be a cup, a ladle or a bowl in your cupboard. The key to following the recipe is to use the same container throughout for measuring. We'll use a standard measuring cup in this example. I will now share with you my recipe for sushi-zu (don't tell anyone . . .)

In a large bowl, combine the sugar and salt. Gradually add the vinegar; I do this in small increments so that by the time I finish adding it, the sugar and salt are completely dissolved.

Place the mixture in a nonreactive storage container, such as plastic, with an airtight lid, add the konbu, cover and allow to age at least for 2 weeks on the counter away from the sun or direct heat. After the aging process is done, you can keep the konbu in the container. Since this is vinegar, you can just keep it on your counter; sushi-zu will keep indefinitely.

---

1 part or 1 cup (200 g) sugar

¼ part or ¼ cup (60 g) sea salt

2 parts or 2 cups (480 ml) rice vinegar

1 piece konbu

HOW TO COOK SUSHI RICE

MAKES 20 OZ (567 G)

Sushi rice is made with short- or medium-grain rice. Rice is critical to making sushi. No matter how good your other ingredients might be, if your rice is not good, your sushi will not be good. That is why sushi chefs take extra care when preparing rice.

How much rice you are going to make will depend on how much sushi you want to make. One cup (180 g) of uncooked rice will make 10 ounces (283 g) of cooked rice. This will give you enough rice to make two *uramaki* (rice-outside rolls), three *hosomaki* (rice-inside rolls) and eight nigiri pieces. In this recipe, we will make 2 cups (360 g) of uncooked rice. After your sushi rice is cooked and mixed, it should have a round, slightly sweet-and-sour taste coming from the sushi-zu. The grains will have little spaces in between them and there shouldn't be any lumps after having mixed the rice and sushi-zu together. The rice grains will be tender but firm.

Let's get to work!

---

2 cups (360 g) uncooked short- or medium-grain rice
2 1/8 cups (510 ml) water, for cooking
7 tbsp (105 ml) Sushi-Zu (page 19)

Washing the Rice

1. In a large bowl, combine the rice with 1 cup (240 ml) of water. Gently massage the rice, putting your hand under it, lifting it up and folding it over. Continue to gently fold the rice in the bowl for 1 minute. You will note that the water will turn milky white. Washing the rice removes surface oil, excess starch, dust and any stale odors. It is very important to do this gently as you do not want to break the grains of rice.

2. Place a mesh colander in your sink to catch any grains of rice that may fall while you are rinsing. Add more water to the bowl of rice until it comes above the level of the rice. Carefully pour the water from the bowl over the colander. Then, add more water to the bowl to cover the rice. Repeat until the water runs clear. I usually teach my students to rinse their rice five or six times. This tends to be enough.

3. Empty the rice into the colander (discarding all the water) and allow it to dry for at least 30 minutes. This equalizes the moisture on the inside and outside. Rice has moisture inside. When we wash it, besides removing dust and dirt from the grains, we also moisturize the rice on the outside to make it equal to the moisture on the inside. This process allows rice to achieve the proper texture after cooking.

(continued)

Cooking the Rice

4. If you are using an electric rice cooker, as shown in the photo, use the measuring cup that came with the cooker to measure both the rice and water for cooking. Cook the rice according to the rice cooker's directions. If you are cooking the rice on a stovetop, in a large pot, bring the rice and 2¹/₈ cups (510 ml) of fresh water to a boil over high heat. Cover, lower the heat to medium and cook for 12 minutes. Then, lower the heat to low and cook for another 8 minutes. Turn off the heat and allow the rice to steam for an additional 20 minutes. The lid must remain on the pot all throughout cooking and steaming (no peeking).

5. Have a large, clean bowl ready. When the rice is finished cooking, transfer it to the bowl. You can also use a traditional hangiri, as shown in the picture.

Seasoning the Rice

6. Next, we are going to work on mixing the rice with the sushi-zu. Mixing sushi rice is one of the most challenging tasks. Ideally, each grain of rice should be coated. To do this, start by carefully pouring the sushi-zu over the rice. To help with this, you can pour the sushi-zu over your rice paddle over the rice.

7. Gently fold the rice with a plastic or wooden rice paddle, so that the vinegar covers each grain of rice. Folding the rice should take no more than 2 minutes. If you don't have a rice paddle, you can use another flat kitchen utensil, such as a nonmetal spatula.

Storing the Rice

8. Wrap any leftover rice in plastic wrap and freeze it. You can keep it in your freezer for up to a month.

9. When you need it, gradually reheat it in a microwave: First, defrost it and then heat for 3 minutes at 50% power, checking its temperature every minute. The heating time might need to be adjusted depending on the power of your microwave. You can reheat the rice in its plastic wrap; this will help keep the moisture in. This is a great way of ensuring there is no waste.

10. Keep heating until the rice reaches a warm body temperature (approximately 100°F [38°C]).

> **CHEF ANDY'S NOTE ON MEASURES:** When cooking rice in a Japanese rice cooker, you may see the line indicators inside the rice cooker in "cups." In Japan, 1 fluid cup is 6 ounces (180 ml), but in the United States, 1 fluid cup is 8 ounces (240 ml). It can be confusing, so make sure to use either Japanese cups or U.S. cups to measure both your rice and water. Don't mix it up, or the results might be a little off. Measuring cups are particularly important when making sushi rice or sauces. When cooking rice or mixing it with the sushi-zu, it's necessary to always have the right amount of each to maintain the proportion of flavor and consistency. Note that the ratio of sushi-zu (vinegar) to rice is 15 percent.

GETTING FAMILIAR WITH FISH AND SEAFOOD

Before you begin to buy fish and seafood, it's good to familiarize yourself with the types of fish you're going to be working with. Here is some info to keep in mind.

MAGURO (TUNA): Sushi bars mostly use four types of tuna: bluefin, bigeye, yellowfin and albacore. The underbelly of bluefin tuna, *toro*, is fatty and oily/buttery in taste. It is the most flavorful and expensive item at a sushi bar. Bigeye and yellowfin tuna have a nice bright red color. Albacore tuna is more of the brownish-red color. Bigeye, yellowfin and albacore tuna can be found as frozen products and are easy to store; they are popular in most Asian markets. Some parts of the tuna are all red. Some parts have white lines running through the filet—connective tissue. The connective tissue can be tough and stringy. To avoid this, be sure your knife is cutting against these white lines at about a 90-degree angle. This will sever the connective tissues, making it pleasant to eat.

SHAKE (SALMON): Salmon is currently one of the most popular seafoods at sushi bars in the world. This is thanks to the development of salmon farming worldwide. Canada, Norway, Chile and many other countries are leaders in this practice. Many fishermen catch wild salmon in oceans or fresh waters. You must be careful because when salmon is caught in the mountains, it might be dangerous to eat raw or in sashimi, since it may contain parasites. People can get very sick when eating freshwater salmon. When visiting your favorite sushi bar, you can ask where your salmon is from. You should always eat sushi at restaurants with very well-educated and professional sushi chefs. To safely eat raw salmon, it should be frozen for at least 1 week. Freezing the salmon will kill the bacteria. After 1 week, defrost the salmon and enjoy.

HAMACHI (YELLOWTAIL): Yellowtail mostly comes from Japan, and it's farmed on the south side of the island, the place with most popular fish farming and with many years of history and quality of fish. You can also find yellowtail that has been farmed at other countries, such as the United States, Mexico and Australia. Yellowtail can be obtained from many wholesalers and distributors in the seafood market in downtown Los Angeles. Some ship all over the United States.

TAI (RED SNAPPER/SEA BREAM): Red snapper is very popular in Japan, and it's known as the king of white fish. Japanese people really appreciate its shape, color and taste and this derives from the meaning of its name in our language. It is mostly known as sea bream in the United States, and it became very popular in the late 1980s—so popular that some people were selling other fish and calling it red snapper. You can break down a whole snapper by following the tutorial on page 35.

UNI (SEA URCHIN): Sea urchin is a very popular delicacy at sushi bars. Even though it is considered harmful for the ecosystem when its population grows, it's hard to catch and then extract the edible part from uni. The golden edible part that we all enjoy has a very buttery texture that almost melts in your mouth. Due to sea urchin's strict kelp diet, its tastes like sweet ocean. Most people, me included, enjoy it best as is. The usage of uni has gotten more creative nowadays. People make uni pasta, uni croquettes and so on. What makes it very particular is that it is pretty much ready to serve after the edible parts have been extracted from the shell; uni is mostly found like this at seafood stores or specialized distributors, since there's not much cutting that needs to be done to it.

IKURA (SALMON EGGS): In my opinion, *ikura* are beautiful as they are. They are a great example of Mother Nature's perfection. However, if we want to consume them, we must follow certain procedures that are explained on page 32, which involves marinating. I always focus on different ways for plating them, since they might come across as challenging for people due to their "liquid form"; in cases like this, the five Japanese colors come into play. Salmon eggs are also great for garnishing, especially white seafood, such as *ika* (squid) or white fish. One popular way of plating ikura is by placing them on top of rice in a *donburi*-style (bowl). You can place a shiso leaf on top of your rice, then add ikura on top, covering the rice, and finish it by adding a little prepared wasabi on top. Another idea is to serve just a little ikura on a small, nice cup or bowl and add some prepared wasabi on top to enjoy the ikura as is.

HOTATE (SCALLOP): Scallop's natural form is perceived as a "big chunk" and that's why we slice it in half or flat when serving it in sashimi or nigiri. This gives the freedom to elevate the dishes and plating can be more delicate and sublime. In terms of pairing, salt and lemon juice are always perfect.

TIPS ON BUYING FISH AND SEAFOOD

Whether you're eating your fish raw or cooked, it must have been handled properly before reaching the store. And, when buying fish for sushi, nigiri or sashimi, it is critically important to know where your seafood comes from, since you are going to be eating it raw. There is no such thing as sushi-grade fish. Keep in mind that for certain fish, freezing them is part of the safety measures to eat them raw. It's important to know how to prep fresh filets, as they could be dangerous to eat if not prepared correctly. Make sure that when you are buying fish filets at a Japanese supermarket, they are meant to be used for sushi or sashimi. Develop a relationship with your retailer and ask them questions about your fish. These are some key points you can look for:

• Some Asian supermarkets will have little labels that say "for sashimi" or "for sushi" on their raw fish filets. Always ask your supplier each time about the specific fish you are purchasing and whether it is safe to eat it raw. Some fish needs to be treated before you can eat it raw. In the case of salmon, your fish supplier will know which filets have been marinated or treated for raw consumption (salmon should be salted and frozen for at least a week; I don't teach you in this book how to do the marinating technique for salmon since it is a slightly more advanced topic).

• Looking at the color of your raw fish might not be enough to know whether it's fresh or not. Some retailers use chemicals that preserves the fish's color, which makes it difficult to know how long it has been sitting on the shelf. I recommend that you obtain your fish from a specialized retailer (online or in person) that is accustomed to selling fish that can be eaten raw.

• When buying a whole fish, you can look at its eyes to determine freshness; they should be clear. A fish's gills should also be bright red. Brown gills means that your fish is old and must be eaten cooked. Fresh fish smells clean like the ocean.

• Always keep your fish as cold as possible. When you are buying fish in person, bring an insulated bag or ice chest for you to carry your fish. While you are preparing it, put it in a tray covered with ice unless you are serving it right away.

• Freshwater fish, such as trout, bass and *unagi* (eel), are generally not meant to be eaten raw in sushi.

• When buying scallops, look for "dry packed" or "chemical free." Scallops are commonly labeled IQF, meaning "individually quick frozen." I'd recommend buying those as this allows you to defrost just what you are using.

PREPARING EBI (SHRIMP)

MAKES 6 SHRIMP

You can buy shrimp frozen at the store. Among some of the major exporters of shrimp are Thailand and Mexico. There are many kinds of shrimp, and they are used in cuisines around the world, making them one of the most popular seafoods. When preparing shrimp for sushi, the variety is not so important since it depends on the local availability. There is a slight flavor difference between kinds, but what matters the most is the size. Shrimp size is measured by the number of shrimp in a pound. The smaller the number, the bigger the shrimp. The most commonly used shrimp size in a sushi bar is 21/25 or 26/30. This means that you get 21 to 25 shrimp per pound or 26 to 30 shrimp per pound, respectively. Most of the time, shrimp is served cooked and prepped in a way that makes it look straight, not curved. To keep the shrimp from curling, we skewer them before boiling. For this technique, we will need six skewers, plus the following:

6 large, unpeeled shrimp

¾ cup (180 ml) rice vinegar, divided

2 tbsp (36 g) salt, plus more for sprinkling

1. Holding a shrimp straight in your left hand, carefully insert a skewer between the shell and the flesh down the center line to the tail.

2. In a saucepan, bring 10 cups (2.4 L) of water to a boil and add ¼ cup (60 ml) of the vinegar and the salt. The salt and vinegar will preserve the flavor and color of the shrimp. Have a bowl of ice water ready.

3. Boil the shrimp for 2 to 3 minutes. Remove from the pot and place in the ice water to stop the cooking.

(continued)

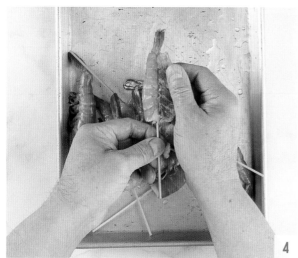

4

5

4. Remove each skewer by rotating it as you are pulling it out of the shrimp. Rotating the skewer detaches it from the flesh and prevents damage to the meat.

5. Peel the shrimp and place horizontally on a cutting board. Using a sharp knife at a 45-degree angle, cut the outer round part of each shrimp tail. This is done for presentation purposes.

6. Position the shrimp on your cutting board with their respective tail away from you and use your knife at a 45-degree angle to cut a little triangular piece from the bottom side of each shrimp. This is done so your shrimp look nicer and more even on your sushi. You can use the cutoff pieces for soup or just eat them.

7. Cut open the underside of each shrimp to butterfly it. Take care not to cut all the way through. Rinse the shrimp under running water. Pat them dry with paper towels and place, cut side up, on a tray or in a bowl.

8. Sprinkle salt on the shrimp and let rest for 20 minutes. Rinse the shrimp under running water. Pat dry with paper towels. The shrimp are now ready to use. If you want to keep the shrimp longer than 1 day, before rinsing them, continue to step 9.

9. Meanwhile, in a medium bowl, combine 10 cups (2.4 L) cold water and the remaining ½ cup (120 ml) of vinegar. Place the salted shrimp in the vinegar solution for 2 minutes. Remove the shrimp and pat dry with paper towels. Wrap the shrimp in clean paper towels and refrigerate overnight. The shrimp will keep for 5 days in the refrigerator. For longer storage, you can wrap them and freeze them. Defrost as needed overnight in the refrigerator.

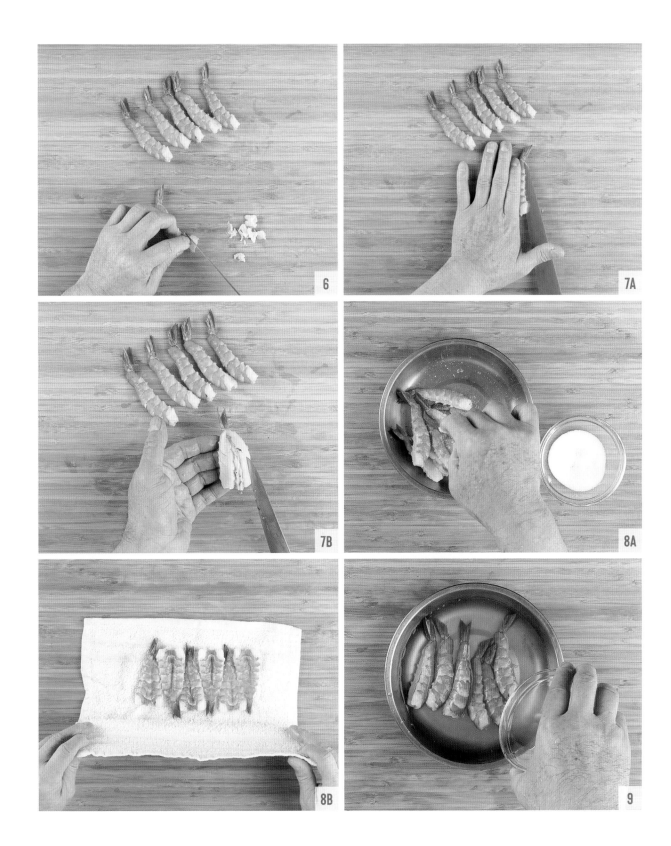

PREPARING TAKO (OCTOPUS)

MAKES 1 OCTOPUS

Most octopus is already cooked and ready to serve. This is convenient, as a whole octopus can be very large. When cutting octopus, we use the technique called *Namigiri* Cut (wave cut). Using the tip of the knife (professional chefs use the yanagi), we slice in a zigzag motion. This makes picking up the octopus with chopsticks much easier and less rubbery in texture. Beginners usually aren't aware of the Namigiri Cut technique, and end up with very thick, chewy slices of octopus in their sushi, but I explain how to perform the cut on page 154. Most of the time, you can find precooked frozen octopus tentacles at the super-market, but I think it's more fun when you get to prepare octopus yourself. The process is not as complicated as you may think, and the result is definitely tastier than the frozen ones.

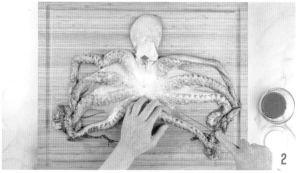

3 tbsp (45 ml) soy sauce

2 tbsp (36 g) salt, plus more for sprinkling

1 octopus

1. Heat 1 gallon (3.8 L) of water in a large pot over high heat. Add the soy sauce and salt to the water.

2. Place your octopus on a cutting board with the bottom of the creature facing upward. Spread the tentacles around the body so you can clearly see the film that appears closer to the body and con-nects the tentacles with one another. With a sharp knife, cut this thin film in the middle until you reach the body. This makes it easier to separate the tentacles after cooking your octopus.

3. Transfer the octopus to a bowl and sprinkle heavily with salt. The salt will help remove the sliminess and bacteria, so be generous. Massage the octopus for at least 10 minutes.

4. Rinse the octopus in a large bowl of fresh water and, using a pair of tongs, dip the octopus into the boiling water and remove it. Dip it into the boiling water at least two more times. We do this so as not to lower the temperature of the water.

5. Place the octopus into the boiling water, lower the heat to a simmer and let cook for 15 minutes. Have ready a bowl of ice water large enough to fit the octopus.

6. Using the tongs, carefully remove the octopus from the pot and place it in the bowl of ice water to cool for at least 5 minutes.

7. The octopus should be a beautiful purple-red color. It is now ready to cut for sushi and sashimi.

3

4A

4B

5

6

7

PREPARING IKURA (SALMON EGGS)

YIELDS 1 CUP (150 G)

Salmon eggs are bought salt packed or marinated when used in sushi making. Marinated salmon eggs are ready to be served, whereas salted eggs need a bit of preparation. You can find salted eggs frozen in most Asian grocery stores. They tend to be on the saltier side, and this technique reduces the saltiness.

DASHI (BONITO STOCK)

1 cup (240 ml) room temperature water

1 oz (28 g) konbu

2 tbsp (30 ml) cold water

¼ oz (7.5 g) bonito flakes

IKURA

4 oz (113 g) salmon eggs

1 tbsp (18 g) salt

½ cup (120 ml) water

½ cup (120 ml) sake, for marinating

MARINADE

¼ cup (60 ml) mirin

¼ cup (60 ml) soy sauce

¼ cup (60 ml) dashi

1. Make the dashi for the marinade: Place the room temperature water and konbu in a pot over medium heat. Bring just to a boil, then remove the konbu right before the water starts boiling. Konbu will become bitter if allowed to boil. Add the cold water, turn off the heat and add the bonito flakes. Allow the bonito flakes to settle to the bottom of the pot. Filter through a paper towel–lined strainer. Allow your dashi to cool down in the fridge before using it. Store in a sealed container in the fridge for no more than 24 hours.

2. Place the salmon eggs in a bowl. Combine the salt and water in a separate bowl and pour it over the salmon eggs. Gently agitate the eggs and remove any broken eggs. These end up usually floating on top of the water when agitated.

3. Pour the eggs into a colander to drain the salt water. Fill a clean bowl with cold water and gently set the colander with the eggs inside the bowl to rinse off any excess salt.

4. Pull the colander out of the bowl and allow the eggs to drain. Rinse the bowl and return the eggs to the clean bowl and cover with the sake. The sake will remove any odor.

5. Let it sit for 1 minute. Pour the sake-marinated eggs in the colander to drain. In the meantime, prepare the marinade: Combine the mirin, soy sauce and dashi in a separate small bowl. If there is time in between washing and marinating the eggs, place the marinade in the refrigerator to keep it cold.

6. Return the eggs to the bowl and add the marinade. Allow to marinate in the fridge for several hours to overnight.

7. You can store them in a covered plastic container in your fridge up to 3 days.

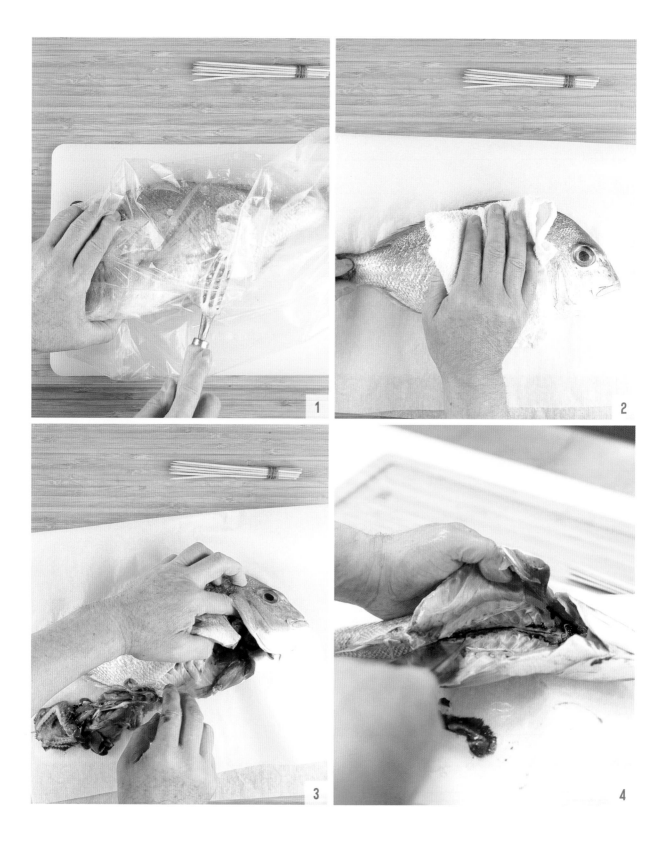

HOW TO BREAK DOWN A WHOLE MEDIUM-SIZED FISH

Fish have different categories and physiognomies and there are different techniques for prepping and working with them depending on those factors. This is just a general introduction on how to cut a whole medium-sized fish that is between 2 and 3 pounds (905 g and 14 kg). Flat fish, such as halibut, use a different technique since their physiognomy is very particular, whereas bigger fish, such as tuna and salmon, need other techniques and tools. With this tutorial, I want to give you the opportunity to break down a whole medium-sized fish . Hopefully, it will awaken an interest to learn more about the right way to do it. Home cooks can use precut filets when making sushi and this is pretty common and convenient, but if you want to challenge yourself and have the knowledge on how to break down a whole fish, you can follow this tutorial.

To cut a whole fish, sharp knives are essential. They will glide through the fish, allowing you to make clean, even cuts. When cutting fish, the knife is always pulled toward you. In this example, we will be breaking down a red snapper, which is a very mild white fish and one of the most popular kinds for making sushi. I enjoy eating it seared with a kitchen torch and brushed with a little Ponzu (page 160). These instructions have been written with a right-handed person in mind. If you are left-handed, just mirror the instructions. You should keep your fish as cold as possible, but not frozen. I highly recommend you obtain and use a scaler. You can buy them online. You could use a metal spoon in a pinch.

1. Begin by scaling the fish. To contain the flying scales, you can place the fish in a plastic bag before you start—it can get very messy if you don't. Break a hole in the plastic bag in the center and insert your scaler through the hole. Hold the fish firmly by the head and pull the scaler up from the tail to the head. When scaling, pay careful attention to the belly and spine, where we will be cutting the fish. Remove the fish from the plastic bag and rinse under cold running water.

2. Pat the fish dry with paper towels or a clean kitchen towel. Place the fish horizontally on a cutting board with the tail pointing to the left. Place newspaper, or any kind of paper, under your fish for the next step, to avoid staining your cutting board with blood.

3. Using a sharp knife, slice open the belly of the fish. Do not insert the knife deeply, as we do not want to damage the internal organs, to avoid spillage and make the cleaning process easier. Here, everything will get a little graphic. There will be some blood surrounding the organs and it will get on your hands. The internal organs are all together in that small cavity we just cut into. Remove the internal organs, wrap them in paper and throw them away. We won't be using them.

4. Open the belly and you will see a white film against the spine of the fish, running from head to tail. This film is covering the bloodline and we want to remove it. Using the point of your knife, slice open the film from head to tail.

(continued)

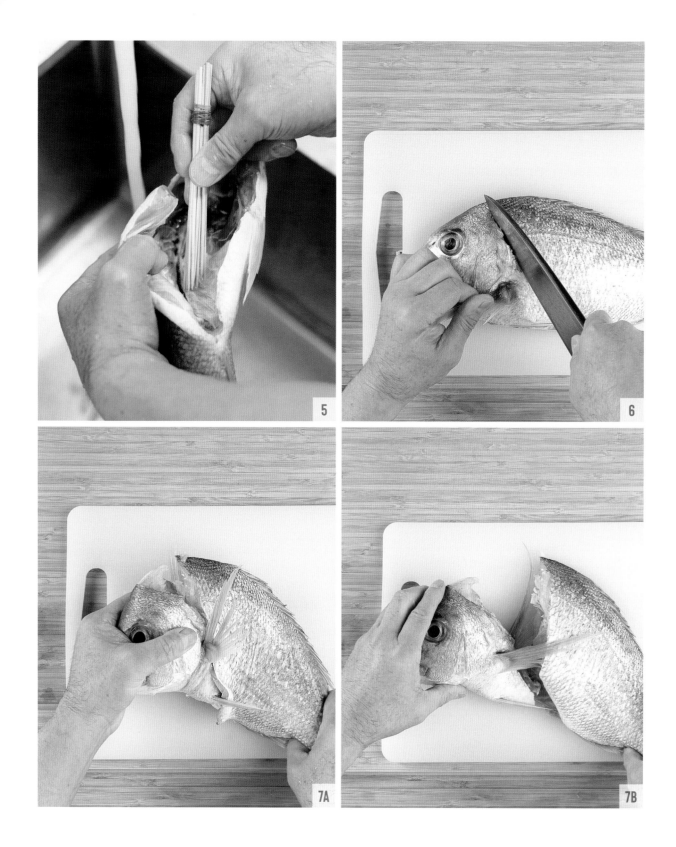

5. For this step, put a bunch of bamboo skewers together and make a little "brush." You can tie one end with a rubber band. I usually wash and reuse the skewers used when making Ebi (page 118). Place the fish under running water and, using your new "brush," clean out the cavity. Make sure the sticks reach the spine as you brush it with them. Put your clean fish on a tray and clean your cutting board before the next step.

6. Place the fish horizontally on the cutting board, with the head pointing to the left. Pick up the pectoral fin (the fin closest to the head) and make a cut from the top of the head down to the belly. Roll the fish over and make the same cut on its other side.

7. Turn the fish over again (head to the left, belly facing you) and grasp the head in your left hand and the tail in your right hand. Pull the head toward you to separate it from the body.

8. Place the fish on the board at a 45-degree angle with the tail pointed toward you. Holding your knife at a 45-degree angle, cut the skin from belly to tail. Holding your knife at a 25-degree angle, insert the knife into the belly about halfway and cut down to the tail. Holding your knife flat, insert the knife into the belly until you reach the middle bone and cut down to the tail.

9. Position the fish horizontally again with the tail toward the left on the cutting board. Make a vertical cut where the tail meets the body, just through enough so that as you cut down, you can feel the middle bone of the fish. Do not cut the tail off or through the middle bone of the fish.

10. Turn the fish over so the back is facing you at a 45-degree angle. Holding your knife at a 45-degree angle, slice through the skin from tail to head.

(continued)

11A

11B

11. Change the angle of the fish to 25 degrees, insert your knife into the fish halfway to the spine and cut from the tail to head. Change the angle of your knife to "flat" and insert all the way to the spine and cut from tail to head.

12. Turn the fish around so its belly is facing you and, with your left hand, lift up the belly. Holding your knife at a 65-degree angle, and using the tip of your knife, cut through the rib bones that hold the filet to the body.

13. After you cut through the last bone, lift the filet out of the body with your left hand.

14. To remove the filet from the other side, turn the remaining fish over and place it on your cutting board at a 45-degree angle, with the tail pointing away from you. Holding your knife at a 45-degree angle, cut the skin from tail to belly. Holding your knife at a 25-degree angle, insert the knife into the belly about halfway and cut down from tail to belly. Holding your knife flat, insert the knife into the belly until you reach the middle bone, then cut down toward you.

15. Position the fish horizontally again with the tail toward the right. Make a vertical cut where the tail meets the body and slice down to the middle bone of the fish. Cut just enough so you cut down and feel the middle bone of the fish. Do not cut the tail off or through the middle bone of the fish.

(continued)

12A 12B 13 14A 14B 15

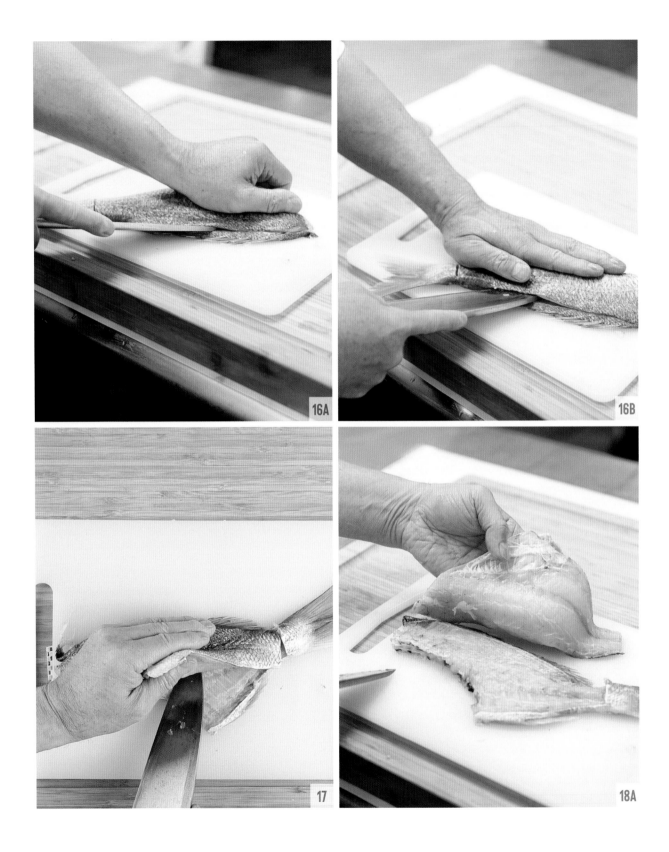

16. Turn the fish around so the top of the fish is facing you at a 45-degree angle. Using your left hand to hold the fish, position your knife at a 45-degree angle and slice through the skin from head to tail. Change the angle to 25 degrees and insert your knife into the fish halfway to the spine and cut from the head to tail. Change the angle of your knife to "flat" and insert all the way to the spine and cut from head to tail.

17. Turn around your fish one more time so its tail is toward the right and, with your left hand, lift the belly up. Holding your knife at a 65-degree angle, and using the tip of your knife, cut through the rib bones that hold the filet to the body.

18. To remove the rib bones from the filets, place the filets, skin side down, with the rib bones toward to your left. Turn your knife blade up and insert the tip under the belly bones to separate them from the filet. Turn the knife over and remove the belly bones with a shallow scooping cut.

19. We are now going to remove the center bones. Place the filet at a 45-degree angle on the cutting board with the narrow part of the filet (the tail) facing you. Cut the filet just to the right of the center bone from head to tail. You now have one filet. Turn the fish around, then cut the filet just to the right again to remove the center bone and make a second filet.

20. At this point, you have a choice to make about skin. If you would like to keep the skin on and eat it, you will need to sear it by fire or by pouring hot water over the skin. Otherwise, you will need to remove it from the filet. Filets for sushi can be kept for up to 1 day in the refrigerator or up to a month in the freezer, wrapped in plastic wrap.

SUSHI ROLLS

My master taught me how to roll when I was 18 years old, back in Japan. Sushi rolls have always been very simple in my country. Even newer roll creations follow the principle of simplicity so you can enjoy the natural flavor of the ingredients. Sushi rolls, as they are known today, are a concept that was born in America. As sushi became more popular, many creative chefs started to add more ingredients and sauces to it. As a side note, I want to point out that for Japanese people, *sushi* refers to nigiri sushi (which we will cover in the next chapter), not rolls.

The creation and popularity of the California Roll (page 61) opened the doors of the world for sushi, and thanks to that, there are now many sushi lovers around the world. Sushi is not only Japanese food anymore; it has become an international food. Who would have thought that street food from 300 years ago in Tokyo would become such an international high-end food today? For me, it is amazing and makes me very happy to see how much sushi has dynamically changed over time.

Sushi rolls started with rice farmers' village celebrations. They used to make special sushi rolls using local ingredients. Japan originally had only a few rolls: the Kappa Maki (page 51), Tekka Maki (page 55)—my favorite—and *futomaki*. Futomaki was a homemade roll with no fish inside and only served in Japan for special occasions, such as New Year's or Obon (a Buddhist festival honoring the dead). In my hometown, futomaki was made with dashi-, soy sauce– and sugar-marinated and cooked *koya* (freeze-dried) tofu, *kanpyō* (a kind of gourd), *tamago* (a sweet omelet) and *mitsuba* (Japanese parsley). It is the most classic roll in Japan. For Setsubun, on February 3 (the day before the beginning of spring in Japan), many sushi bars have sales on *maki* (layered, rolled up and then sliced) sushi rolls. The tradition is that when you eat the whole roll silently, your new year will go in the right direction and a year of happiness will come to you. It is a very special seasonal sushi ceremony in Japan.

Sushi rolls give the opportunity for people who don't eat raw fish to enjoy this creative and affordable food. I think that you can master roll making in about two months if you put your heart into it. You don't need to have a lot of professional sushi skills to make sushi rolls. However, when making or creating sushi rolls, it is very important to think about what your guest's favorite ingredients are. You always want to make their sushi experience memorable. That is the hardest part for me when I am creating new rolls.

In this chapter, I will share some very popular special roll recipes, such as the famous California Roll (page 61) and the vegetarian favorite Kappa Maki (Cucumber Roll; page 51). Even though these recipes are popular, I like to add my personal touch. One example is my Signature Roll (page 90), which is a new take on the staple spicy tuna roll. Tuna is one of my favorite fish to put in a roll, so make sure to try those recipes. Tuna is a rich fish that can produce a unique experience depending on the part you are using. The textures of the different parts of tuna make it very versatile and you can make unique recipes with each one of them.

Remember to use my six-step techniques for spreading the rice and it should be easy to make the rolls ahead. People always ask me how many rolls I have made in my life. I think I've reached my 2 million rolls milestone and am finally doing better when rolling. One of my craziest roll-making stories is when I made my "mega roll" at the Sushi Chef Institute for an event. That gigantic 30-foot (6-m) and 60-pound (27-kg) roll went all over social media and reached over 20 million people. I needed the help of about 15 sushi chefs to be able to make it. I wanted to introduce sushi rolls to the public in an entertaining way. It was one of the biggest surprises of my life. I'm looking forward to continuing to create exciting new rolls in the future.

Roll making might be frustrating in the beginning and your rolls may not be that great looking, but you will only get better. I invite you to take pictures of your rolls from day one and continue doing so every time you make sushi. You will see how much you've improved when you browse through your images. It takes time to be good at making sushi, but I believe this book will help you achieve that goal!

GETTING STARTED

Before we start to roll sushi, we need to set up our work area. Gather a cutting board, makisu (bamboo mat), plastic wrap, knife, a wet towel and *temizu* (how to make this follows) prior to getting out your ingredients.

WORKING WITH TEMIZU

If you have visited a sushi bar, you may have noticed the chef periodically dipping their fingers in a little bowl of liquid. They are dipping their hands in temizu. Temizu is used to keep your hands moist while rolling sushi. It also acts as sanitizer because it contains rice vinegar. These instructions have been written with a right-handed person in mind. If you are left-handed, simply mirror the instructions.

---

1 cup (240 ml) cold water

1 tbsp (15 ml) rice vinegar

Ice cubes, as needed

1. To make temizu, place the cold water in a nonreactive container and add the rice vinegar. Mix and keep some in a bowl near your rolling station. If your water starts to get warm, add some ice cubes to it to keep it cold. This will help prevent the sushi rice from sticking to your fingers.

2. To use the temizu, dip the fingers of your right hand in the temizu container. Rub your wet fingers on your left hand. Then, push the excess water off your hands by taking your right hand and rubbing it down the length of your left hand. You want your hands to be moist, not wet. This process is performed by chefs to shake off the excess of water. If you use a towel, you will accelerate the drying process and it's very possible that rice will stick to them faster. You want a very thin layer of moisture coating your hands whenever handling sushi rice.

WORKING WITH NORI

When using nori in sushi rolls, we cut a single 7½ x 8–inch (19 x 20–cm) sheet in half to be 7½ x 4 inches (19 x 10 cm) before beginning to make our roll. Nori usually comes with vertical lines that you can see if you hold your sheet against the light. Use those vertical lines as reference; fold your nori sheet in half along the lines and cut it carefully with a knife.

Nori has a shiny side and a rough side. Rice is always placed on the rough side. Crispiness is most important for nori. When you open a new package, always reseal it to keep the nori dry. If you are not going to be using it all, store the remainder of the package in the freezer. When you need it, simply remove from the freezer and individually reheat the sheets in the toaster oven at 350°F (180°C) for 5 seconds to make them crispy again.

You are now ready to use nori to work with your Sushi Rice (page 20) and create rolls and nigiri.

HOSOMAKI (RICE-INSIDE ROLLS)

Rice-inside rolls will be a test of willpower. Usually made with one major filling ingredient, aside from the rice, the temptation to add more can be overwhelming. Resist the temptation. Too much inside and the roll will not close. So, we will be practicing restraint when making these rolls. Hosomaki are made with 3 ounces (85 g) of sushi rice and are a real test of a sushi chef's skill.

Rice-inside rolls are the most popular kind in Japan. Since the nori is outside, this is what you will taste first, and you will be finding the flavors of the ingredients inside little by little until you reach the center of the roll. At the end, you feel the combination of all the ingredients and their harmony. These instructions have been written with a right-handed person in mind. If you are left-handed, just mirror the instructions. Whenever handling sushi rice, remember to use temizu (see page 44). Dip your fingers in the temizu whenever you feel the rice is beginning to stick to your hands or is becoming hard to work with. Ideally, the temperature of your rice should be body temperature, about 98°F (37°C).

(continued)

HOW TO ROLL HOSOMAKI

1. Place your nori on a makisu (bamboo mat), rough side up. Pick up the 3 ounces (85 g) of prepared Sushi Rice (page 20) in your left hand and gently shape it into a log half the length of a nori sheet.

2. Place the rice on the center of the right edge of the nori and, using the first three fingers of your right hand, gently push the rice across the nori while pulling the rice with your left hand.

3. You should have a line of rice across the center of the sheet of nori.

4. Place your left hand on the edge the nori—this will keep the rice from going off the nori—and, using your thumb on your right hand, push some the rice toward the top left corner of the nori, stopping ½ inch (1.3 cm) from the top.

5. Using the first three fingers of your right hand, pull some rice down to the bottom left side of the nori.

6. Place your right hand on the right edge of the nori and, using the thumb on your left hand push the rice toward the top right corner of the nori, stopping ½ inch (1.3 cm) from the top, in the same place as the right side.

7. Using the fingers of your left hand, pull the rice down to the bottom right corner of the nori.

8. Using your thumbs, push some of the rice in the center toward the top of the nori stopping at the same ½ inch (1.3 cm) line from the top.

9. Using the fingers of both hands, pull some of the rice down the center of the nori to the bottom edge.

10. Place your filling in the center of the rice. If you have multiple ingredients, lay them side by side in a long, thin line spread evenly, going all the way to the edges horizontally, not vertically. You still want space to be able to roll and close your sushi roll.

11. Use your left thumb to lift the makisu upward by 90 degrees while your fingers hold the filling in place.

12. With your right hand, guide the makisu over the filling until the rice from the top side meets the rice on the lower side, and pinch the roll gently. Make sure your ingredients are nice and tight when doing this step.

13. With your right hand, pick up the edge of the makisu and continue to roll until the nori portions meet and pinch again to shape and help seal the roll.

14. Remove the makisu and place the roll, seam side down, on a cutting board. It is now ready to be cut. Dip the tip of a sharp knife in your temizu and hold up the knife, allowing the water to run down the length of the blade. Cut the roll into six pieces wiping your knife on a clean, wet towel as needed.

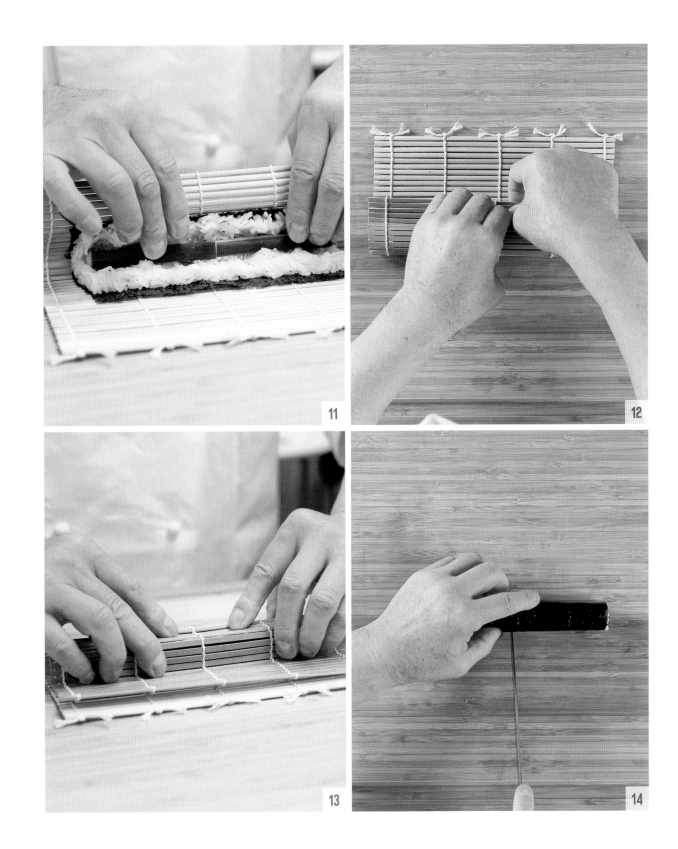

KAPPA MAKI (CUCUMBER ROLL)

MAKES 1 ROLL

This is one of two of the most classic rolls in Japan, named Kappa after an old Japanese monster's name that eventually became a popular manga character. The reason to use Kappa's name for this roll is that this character's favorite food is cucumber. It has become the favorite and most popular roll among vegans and vegetarians. In this recipe, I will also teach you how to cut cucumbers for sushi rolls, which is the method used for all the sushi roll recipes in this book that contain cucumber.

2 pieces cucumber (see below for cutting technique)

½ (7½ x 8" [19 x 20–cm]) sheet nori

3 oz (85 g) Sushi Rice (page 20)

Sesame seeds

1 tsp wasabi paste, for serving

1 tbsp (15 g) pickled sushi ginger, for serving

1. Cut one whole cucumber so it is half the full length of a sheet of nori. The easiest way to do this is to fold a sheet of nori in half lengthwise and use that as a guide. Next, cut the cucumber around the core, so you have four pieces. Then, cut each of the four pieces into pencil-thick sticks. Remember you want to have skin on your cucumber to add that crunch to your roll, to create contrast with the softness of your rice. When cutting cucumber, we cut around the seedy core to achieve this.

2. Position your nori sheet horizontally on a makisu (bamboo mat) and spread the rice on the nori sheet according to the directions on page 47 for Hosomaki (Rice-Inside Rolls). Sprinkle some sesame seeds over the rice.

3. Place the cucumber pieces in the middle of the nori. Roll up and mold the roll with the bamboo mat according to the directions on page 47.

4. Cut the roll into six equal pieces. Put them on a serving plate and add the wasabi and pickled sushi ginger to the plate.

1A

1C

1B

1D

AVOCADO ROLL

MAKES 1 ROLL

Avocado is not a Japanese vegetable, but it has become a very important one when making sushi. It all started with the California Roll (page 61) and became a very popular ingredient because of its rich and creamy flavor. The way avocado easily blends with other ingredients made it a favorite. Also, avocado is generally very popular in many countries. It allows vegans and vegetarians to enjoy sushi as well. In this recipe, I will also teach you how to cut avocado for sushi rolls, which is the method used for all the sushi roll recipes in this book that contain avocado.

2 slices avocado (see below for cutting technique)
½ (7½ x 8" [19 x 20–cm]) sheet nori
3 oz (85 g) Sushi Rice (page 20)
1 tsp wasabi paste, for serving
1 tbsp (15 g) pickled sushi ginger, for serving

1. Take an avocado and cut it in half lengthwise. Carefully remove the pit by inserting the bottom corner of the knife blade into the pit and twisting the knife. Cut each half in half lengthwise, then cut each half in half lengthwise again to create a thin wedge. Remove the peel. The avocado is now ready to be added inside rolls. If you would like to place it on top of rolls, make sure you cut thinner slices, about ⅛ inch (3 mm) thick.

2. Place your nori sheet horizontally on a makisu (bamboo mat) and spread the rice on the nori according to the directions on page 47 for Hosomaki (Rice-Inside Rolls).

3. Take your avocado slices and place the pieces in the middle of the nori.

4. Roll up and mold the roll with the makisu according to the directions on page 47.

5. Cut the roll into six equal pieces. Put them on a serving plate and add the wasabi and pickled sushi ginger to the plate.

TEKKA MAKI (TUNA ROLL)

MAKES 1 ROLL

This roll is the oldest roll in Japan. It is believed to have been around for over 200 years. Originally, it was very popular in gambling dens and eventually in casinos, and so it came to be called a casino roll in Japan. Its popularity was because people could "touch" tuna sushi with their hands, thanks to a sushi chef who used nori to wrap it.

---

1 oz (28 g) tuna (sliced using the Sogigiri Neta Cut, page 142)

½ (7½ x 8" [19 x 20–cm]) sheet nori

3 oz (85 g) Sushi Rice (page 20)

1 tsp wasabi paste, for serving

1 tbsp (15 g) pickled sushi ginger, for serving

1. Cut the sliced tuna into strips about ¼ inch (6 mm) thick and as long as your nori sheet. If your fish slices are not long enough, you can place as many pieces as needed for this side by side.

2. Place your nori sheet horizontally on a makisu (bamboo mat) and spread the rice on the nori according to the directions on page 47 for Hosomaki (Rice-Inside Rolls).

3. Place a couple of pieces of tuna in the middle of the nori. Roll up and mold the roll with the makisu according to the directions on page 47.

4. Cut the roll into six equal pieces. Put them on a serving plate and add the wasabi and pickled sushi ginger to the plate.

URAMAKI (RICE-OUTSIDE ROLLS)

Rice-outside rolls are the most popular kind beyond Japan. These allow you to be more creative and use more ingredients in and on your sushi rolls. You will taste the rice more since it's what touches your tongue first. These instructions have been written with a right-handed person in mind. If you are left-handed, just mirror the instructions. Whenever handling sushi rice, remember to use temizu (see page 44). Dip your fingers in the temizu whenever you feel the rice is beginning to stick to your hands or is becoming hard to work with. The temperature of your rice should ideally be body temperature, about 98°F (37°C).

HOW TO ROLL URAMAKI

1. Place your nori on a cutting board, rough side up. Pick up 4 ounces (115 g) of prepared Sushi Rice (page 20) in your left hand and gently shape it into a log half the length of a nori sheet.

2. Place the rice on the center on the right edge of the nori and, using the first three fingers of your right hand, gently push the rice across the nori while pulling the rice with your left hand. You should have a line of rice across the center of the sheet of nori.

3. Place your left hand on the edge of the nori (this will keep the rice from going off the nori) and, using your thumb, push some the rice to the top left corner of the nori.

4. Using the first three fingers of your right hand, pull some rice down to the bottom left side of the nori.

5. Place your right hand on the right edge of the nori. Using the thumb on your left hand, push the rice to the top corner of the nori.

6. Using the fingers of your left hand, pull the rice down to the bottom right corner of the nori.

7. Using your thumbs, push some of the rice in the center to the top of the nori.

8. Using the fingers of both hands, pull some of the rice down the center of the nori to the bottom edge. The amount of rice you are using should be enough to cover the nori evenly.

(continued)

9. Sprinkle some sesame seeds, if using, on the rice. Flip the nori over and now you are ready to prepare any rice outside roll.

10. Place your ingredients, side by side, in the center of the nori, being sure that the ingredients are spread evenly and go all the way to the edges horizontally, not vertically. You still want space to be able close your sushi roll.

11. Slide your thumbs under the edge of the nori while holding the other ingredients with your fingers.

12. Roll the edge of the nori just over the fillings while tucking the fillings firmly but gently underneath the nori, so that your ingredients are nice and tight. Continue to roll until the roll is closed.

13. Now, we will shape our roll for presentation. Place the piece of plastic wrap over the closed-up roll.

14. Place a makisu (bamboo mat) on the plastic wrap and line up the right edge of the makisu with the right edge of the roll. Gently press the makisu to shape the roll with your fingers.

15. Gently press the makisu to shape the roll with your left hand while holding your right hand against the right edge of the roll. This will keep your ingredients from slipping out.

16. Press the makisu to shape the roll with your right hand while holding your left hand against the left edge of the roll. This will keep your ingredients in place.

17. Now, we are ready to cut. Remove the makisu but leave the plastic wrap in place—we'll need it in a minute. Using a sharp knife, cut the roll into eight equal pieces. Place the makisu over the roll and reshape the roll. Remove the makisu and the plastic wrap and enjoy your roll.

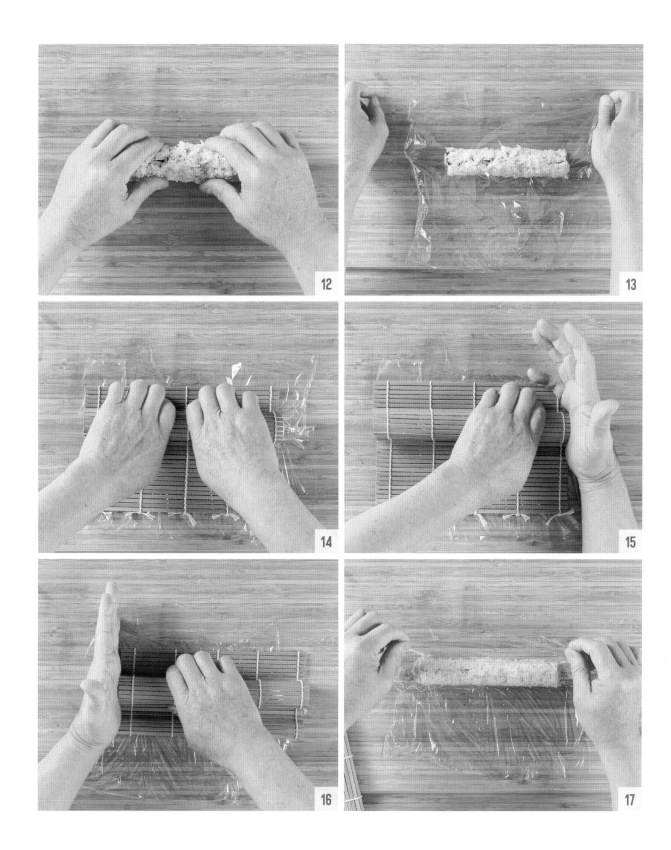

CALIFORNIA ROLL

MAKES 1 ROLL

This classic roll is a great one to practice your rolling skills with. California rolls are filled with three ingredients: avocado, cucumber and *kanikama* (imitation crab). One of the stories behind this popular roll is that in the 1960s in Little Tokyo in Los Angeles, the sushi chef of famous Japanese restaurant Tokyo Kaikan created a special roll that would change the sushi industry forever. This roll was made using California's local, popular ingredients: crabmeat, cucumbers and avocado. This helped the sushi boom to come at the 1984 Los Angeles Olympics. This is a great introductory roll to sushi as it contains no raw fish. You can purchase kanikama online or in most Asian supermarkets.

½ (7½ x 8" [19 x 20–cm]) sheet nori

4 oz (115 g) Sushi Rice (page 20)

Sesame seeds

½ tsp Kanikama Sauce (page 158)

2 pieces cucumber (see page 51 for cutting technique)

2 pieces avocado (see page 52 for cutting technique)

1 stick imitation crab

1 tsp wasabi paste, for serving

1 tbsp (15 g) pickled sushi ginger, for serving

1. Place your nori sheet horizontally on a cutting board, rough side up, and spread the rice through the nori sheet according to the directions on page 57 for Uramaki (Rice-Outside Rolls). Make sure the rice covers the nori completely.

2. Sprinkle sesame seeds over the rice and flip over the sheet so the rice is upside down, and the bare nori is facing up.

3. Spread the kanikama sauce along the middle of the nori.

4. Place the cucumber and avocado pieces in the middle of the nori. Add the imitation crab stick as well in the same place. You want the avocado, cucumber and imitation crab to all be as close as possible, while still lying flat. If your pieces are on the larger side, you can stack the crab on top of the cucumber and avocado, but keep them side by side if possible.

5. Roll up and mold the roll with a makisu (bamboo mat) according to the directions on page 57.

6. Cut the roll into eight equal pieces. Put them on a serving plate and add the wasabi and pickled sushi ginger to the plate.

SPICY TUNA ROLL

MAKES 1 ROLL

In Japanese sushi, the only spicy taste we have is wasabi, a.k.a. Japanese horseradish. With the expansion and popularity of sushi around the world and the great variety of spices and sauces, sushi chefs created the now very popular spicy sauce used in this roll. Many sushi lovers enjoy spicy rolls with mayonnaise-based sauces. This roll has become one of the world's most favorite rolls.

2 oz (55 g) tuna

Spicy Mayo (page 158)

½ (7½ x 8" [19 x 20–cm]) sheet nori

Sesame seeds

4 oz (115 g) Sushi Rice (page 20)

2 pieces avocado (optional; see page 52 for cutting technique)

2 pieces cucumber (see page 51 for cutting technique)

1 tsp wasabi paste, for serving

1 tbsp (15 g) pickled sushi ginger, for serving

1. For this roll, you can use leftover pieces of tuna that have been chopped or cut into very small dice. Either way, you'll want to cut your tuna into small dice before starting.

2. Place the tuna in a bowl and gradually add the Spicy Mayo until the mixture reaches your desired level of spiciness. (If you have any spicy tuna leftovers, consume them. I don't recommend storing for more than 24 hours.)

3. Place the nori on a makisu (bamboo mat) and spread the rice as shown on page 57 for Uramaki (Rice-Outside Rolls). Sprinkle with sesame seeds and flip it over so the rice is now on the bottom and the nori side faces up.

4. Place the avocado (if using) in a line in the middle of the nori. Place the cucumber next to the avocado. Place the spicy tuna in a line on top of the avocado and cucumber.

5. Roll up the roll according to the directions on page 57.

6. Cut the roll into eight equal pieces. Put them on a serving plate and add the wasabi and pickled sushi ginger to the plate.

CHEF ANDY'S NOTE: Spicy mayonnaise can be used with almost any fish. Popular choices are scallops, salmon and yellowtail. This is a great way to use leftover pieces of fish.

RAINBOW ROLL

MAKES 1 ROLL

This roll was also born in Little Tokyo in Los Angeles as an evolution of the California Roll (page 61), which is used as a base for this roll. This new roll places five different types of sliced fish diagonally on top of the California roll; *rainbow* refers to the color contrast of the different fish. This beautiful-looking roll was creative and appetizing, making it a very popular roll right away. In Japan, we have a *tazuna* roll that looks very similar to the American rainbow roll, but in Japan, it resembles the strands of fiber that make a rope. The fish on top can be changed, so use this recipe as a guide.

---

1 California Roll (page 61), uncut

1 slice tuna (cut using the Sogigiri Neta Cut, page 106)

1 slice salmon (cut using the Sogigiri Neta Cut, page 106)

1 slice white fish (halibut, yellowtail or sea bass; cut using the Sogigiri Neta Cut, page 106)

1 shrimp (see page 27 for prep instructions)

5 pieces thinly sliced avocado

Your favorite sauce (see The Sauce chapter), for serving

1 tsp wasabi paste, for serving

1 tbsp (15 g) pickled sushi ginger, for serving

1. Place the California Roll horizontally on a cutting board. Starting from the left side, place the first piece of fish over the roll at an angle. Next, place a slice of avocado next to the first fish. Continue alternating fish and avocado, adding the shrimp as the last piece of the roll. Cover the roll in plastic wrap and gently shape with a makisu (bamboo mat). Cut the roll into eight equal pieces.

2. Reshape with the makisu while the pieces are still next to each other. Remove the plastic wrap and place the roll on your plate. Use your favorite sauce to decorate the plate. Add the wasabi and pickled sushi ginger to the plate.

TEMPURA SHRIMP & AVOCADO ROLL

MAKES 1 ROLL

While I was working at the Culinary Council for Holland America Cruises, I was asked to come up with a signature roll. I wanted to create something that followed my philosophy of simplicity and limited the amount of ingredients. I incorporated tempura shrimp inside because many people enjoy it worldwide; even in Japan, it's vastly consumed. Then, I added sliced avocado on top for a creamy texture that would pair beautifully with a sweet sauce. It was very successful, and it still is part of Holland America's menu today. This is also a great roll for people new to sushi, as it contains no raw fish.

We will also learn how to make tempura shrimp in this recipe. Tempura was said to have been brought to Japan by the Portuguese in the sixteenth century. The story goes that Portuguese fishermen were not fond of raw fish, so they fried theirs.

There are two key elements to making good tempura. One is cold ingredients. Refrigerate all your ingredients, even your flour, so they are as cold as possible. The second is to not overmix your batter. For best results, mix your batter with chopsticks. Lumps of flour are okay! The consistency should be similar to melted ice cream. Tempura shrimp, when eaten fresh, has a crispy texture on the exterior, and as you bite into it, you will feel a thin, soft layer closer to the shrimp. This golden treat is highly addictive, thanks to the reaction between the batter and the oil. The taste is light and crispy, very different from just regular fried shrimp.

TEMPURA SHRIMP

2 large shrimp (see page 27 for prep technique)

Neutral oil, for frying

1 large egg, cold

1 cup (240 ml) sparkling water, ice cold

1 cup (125 g) all-purpose flour, plus more for dredging

ROLL

4 oz (115 g) Sushi Rice (page 20)

½ (7½ x 8" [19 x 20–cm]) sheet nori

Sesame seeds

2 pieces avocado, (see page 52 for cutting technique)

Sushi sauce (see page 15) or your favorite sauce, for decoration

1 tsp wasabi paste, for serving

1 tbsp (15 g) pickled sushi ginger, for serving

(continued)

1

MAKE THE TEMPURA SHRIMP

1. Peel the shrimp and force the excess water out of the tail by using the back of your knife: While applying a little downward pressure, drag the knife to the end of the tail. Shrimp tails hold water in little pockets at the very end of them. When squishing these ends of the tail with the back of your knife, you will see the water come out. This is important, because excess water can cause the oil to spatter.

2. Devein the shrimp by slicing along the top of the shrimp and removing the black line. Turn the shrimp on its back and make five cuts at an angle across the belly. Turn the shrimp back over and press down to flatten the shrimp. While pressing down, squeeze gently until you feel fibers break. Continue to break the fibers and stretch the shrimp. Place the stretched shrimp on paper towels to dry them.

3. Heat 1 inch (2.5 cm) of oil in a deep skillet to 350°F (180°C). The ideal temperature for frying tempura is between 330 and 360°F (166 and 182°C).

4. Beat the egg in a small bowl and add to the cold sparkling water. Sparkling water is essential in this recipe so as to enhance your experience. The carbon dioxide in it makes the batter crispier when fried. Regular water is commonly used, but I definitely recommend trying my method. Place the flour in a separate bowl. Gradually add the egg mixture to the flour, mixing gently with chopsticks. Do not overmix the batter. Lumps are okay.

2A

2B

5. Dredge the shrimp in the extra flour and then dip the flour-dusted shrimp in the batter. Lay the shrimp in the hot oil and cook for 2 minutes. Tempura cooks quickly, so keep an eye on the shrimp. Cooked shrimp will have a white color underneath and an orange and sometimes red color on top. Once you start spotting that orange color showing through the golden flakes, your shrimp will be ready inside. Remove the cooked shrimp from the pan and drain on a rack. Leftovers can be stored in the refrigerator for 2 days or frozen; reheat in the oven until crispy and heated through.

LET'S MAKE OUR ROLL!

6. Place the rice on the nori as shown on page 57 for Uramaki (Rice-Outside Rolls). Sprinkle with sesame seeds and flip over. Place the two fried shrimp, end to end, on the center of the nori with the tails hanging over the edge of the nori. Roll up the roll by hand according to the directions on page 57.

7. Gently press the avocado pieces on top and spread it to the length of the roll. Cover with plastic wrap. Use the makisu to gently mold the avocado to the roll. Remove the makisu, but leave the plastic wrap and cut the roll into eight equal pieces.

8. Place the makisu back on the roll to reshape it. Remove the makisu and the plastic wrap. Transfer to a serving plate and lay the ends of the roll so the shrimp tails are pointing upward in the air.

9. Decorate the plate with a drizzle of your choice of sauce and add wasabi and pickled sushi ginger to the plate.

5

CHEF ANDY'S NOTES: You can use this same technique for making tempura vegetables and other ingredients as well.

You can also use this batter to make *tenkasu* (crunchy tempura flakes), which we will use in other sushi roll recipes in this book. Tenkasu is made by dipping your fingertips in the tempura batter and drizzling the batter over the hot oil. Once cooked, remove the flakes from the hot oil and drain on paper towels. They take 10 to 15 seconds to cook and will turn a light golden brown color when done. These crunchy tempura flakes can be used to cover the outside of a sushi roll, offering a contrasting texture. These are best when made fresh when you are making tempura, as they can become greasy if you try to store them.

SEARED SALMON ROLL

MAKES 1 ROLL

It is very common to consume raw fish daily in Japan, but not in other countries. That is why the Japanese technique *aburi* (searing) started to be used in sushi. When a sushi chef uses a kitchen torch to sear the raw fish, people unaccustomed to raw food feel more compelled to eat it. This is still a new generation food overseas. By understanding the cultural differences, sushi chefs create and use other techniques, such as searing, to make our customers more comfortable. Since most people enjoy salmon, this roll was created so anybody could enjoy it. It is warm and hearty while still providing that sushi experience.

1 California Roll (page 61), uncut

6 slices salmon (cut using the Sogigiri Neta Cut, page 106)

Spicy Mayo (page 158)

8 capers, rinsed and drained

Red onion, sliced thinly and washed (see note)

1 tsp wasabi paste, for serving

1 tbsp (15 g) pickled sushi ginger, for serving

1. Place the California roll horizontally on a cutting board. Starting from the left, lay the salmon on top of the roll at an angle. Cover with plastic wrap and shape with a makisu (bamboo mat). Cut the roll into eight pieces. Shape again with the makisu. Remove the plastic wrap and place your roll on a heat-resistant tray. Using a kitchen torch, gently sear the salmon for 20 to 30 seconds, moving your torch throughout the roll. Searing times are subjective to your taste so you can always sear to your likeness.

2. Transfer the roll to the serving plate and place a small dot of spicy mayo on top of each piece. Place a caper on top of the mayo and top the entire roll with the washed red onion. Add the wasabi and pickled sushi ginger to the plate.

CHEF ANDY'S NOTE: Washing onions in water will mellow the onion flavor but keep the crunchy texture, making them an ideal garnish. To wash the onions, slice them as thinly as possible. Place them in a strainer and place the strainer in a bowl. Run fresh water over the onions for a few minutes to mellow the flavor.

VEGAN VEGETABLE ROLL

MAKES 1 ROLL

Some people are not able to eat certain things due to their culture, religious beliefs or other dietary restrictions. This roll has been created to give people who cannot eat sushi with fish the opportunity to enjoy rolls as well. Vegetables are an important part of Japanese food culture, so creating a beautiful, healthy and tasty vegetable option is a joy for a sushi chef. You'll love the fresh, earthy flavors in this vibrant vegan roll.

1 red bell pepper (mini bell peppers are good for this)

1 yellow bell pepper (mini bell peppers are good for this)

1 shiitake mushroom

1 slice eggplant

1 slice zucchini

1 tbsp (15 ml) grapeseed oil, divided

4 oz (115 g) Sushi Rice (page 20)

½ (7½ x 8" [19 x 20–cm]) sheet nori

2 pieces avocado (see page 52 for cutting technique)

2 pieces cucumber (see page 51 for cutting technique)

1 stalk asparagus, blanched and cooled

1 tbsp (15 ml) balsamic glaze

Freshly ground black pepper, for sprinkling

1 tsp wasabi paste, for serving

1 tbsp (15 g) pickled sushi ginger, for serving

1. Slice the vegetables: When slicing the bell peppers, shiitake, eggplant and zucchini, remember these are going on the outside of the roll. You want to slice them thinly, so they are flexible, and at an angle that is longer than a straight slice, about 1 inch (2.5 cm) wide and 2 inches (5 cm) long.

2. In a skillet over medium heat, heat 1 teaspoon of the grapeseed oil. Add the sliced bell pepper, mushroom, eggplant and zucchini slices to the skillet and grill for 1 to 2 minutes, or until they soften. Mushrooms tend to take a little longer than most vegetables with high water content. Set your vegetables aside and let them cool down for 5 minutes before putting them on your roll.

3. Place the rice on the nori according to the directions on page 57 and flip the nori over. Place the avocado, cucumber and asparagus on the nori. Roll up your roll according to the directions on page 57.

4. Starting from the left, place your sautéed vegetables, one by one, on the roll at a slight angle, using the bell peppers to provide color between the other vegetables. Cover the roll with plastic wrap and shape with a makisu (bamboo mat). Remove the makisu, leaving the plastic wrap, then cut the roll into eight equal pieces. Place on a plate and drizzle the remaining 2 teaspoons (10 ml) of grapeseed oil and balsamic glaze over the roll. Sprinkle the roll with black pepper and add the wasabi and pickled sushi ginger to the plate.

TUNA DRAGON ROLL

MAKES 1 ROLL

This roll is also a sibling of the California Roll (page 61), which is used as a base for it. It is named "dragon" because of the red tuna slices used on top of it. It aims to re-create a Chinese dancing dragon on your plate.

1 California Roll (page 61), uncut

6 slices tuna (cut using the Sogigiri Neta Cut, page 106)

2 tbsp (30 ml) Spicy Mayo (page 158)

1 tsp wasabi paste, for serving

1 tbsp (15 g) pickled sushi ginger, for serving

1. Place the California Roll horizontally on a cutting board. Starting from the left, place a piece of tuna at a slight angle over the roll. Continue to place the fish over the roll until it is covered. Lay a piece of plastic wrap over the roll and shape with a makisu (bamboo mat). Remove the makisu, leaving the plastic wrap in place, and cut the roll into eight equal pieces. Reshape the roll with the makisu while the plastic wrap is still on.

2. Remove the makisu and plastic wrap, then place the roll on a plate and decorate. When I make this roll, I place a dot of spicy mayo on top of each piece. Add the wasabi and pickled sushi ginger to the plate.

PHILADELPHIA ROLL

MAKES 1 ROLL

As its name says, this roll was born in Philadelphia. It was created by female sushi chef Madame Saito whose clientele was mostly Jewish, and aimed to mimic the flavors of a bagel with cream cheese and smoked salmon. These ingredients never would have been used in a traditional Japanese restaurant. However, the popularity of these ingredients for breakfast inspired this sushi chef to bring Japanese and American culture together. I like to put some other special ingredients in this roll to elevate this unique, flavorful experience. This is a great roll for people new to sushi as it can be made with smoked or raw salmon, as you prefer.

½ (7½ x 8" [19 x 20–cm]) sheet nori

4 oz (115 g) Sushi Rice (page 20)

Sesame seeds

1 oz (28 g) cream cheese, cut into sticks like cucumber (see page 51 for technique)

2 pieces cucumber (see page 51 for cutting technique)

1 tsp capers, rinsed and drained

2 slices red onion (optional)

2 oz (55 g) smoked or raw salmon, cut into thin strips

1 tsp wasabi paste, for serving

1 tbsp (15 g) pickled sushi ginger, for serving

1. Place the nori on a makisu (bamboo mat) and spread the rice as shown on page 57 for Uramaki (Rice-Outside Rolls). Sprinkle with sesame seeds and flip it over so the rice is now on the bottom and the nori side faces up.

2. Place the cream cheese on the center of the nori. Place the cucumber next to the cream cheese. Place the capers on the cream cheese and gently press them into the cream cheese. (This prevents them from rolling away.) Add the red onion (if using). Place the salmon next to the capers and close the roll according to the directions on page 57.

3. Cut the roll into eight equal pieces. Put them on a serving plate and add the wasabi and sliced pickled ginger to the plate.

SALMON SKIN ROLL

MAKES 1 ROLL

In Japan, we have a *mottainai* culture. This means that we try our best to have as little waste as possible. In Japanese cuisine, this is achieved by reinventing and recycling ingredients from leftovers and creating new dishes with it. Salmon skin can be saved to create new dishes. It is very tasty when grilled. It has all the flavor of the salmon and a great crunchiness. Filled with kaiware, yamagobo and cucumber, the crunchy contrast makes it great for hand rolls as well. I like to use bonito flakes outside of the roll for the customer to feel the umami in their mouth and it also makes it look nice.

---

1 tbsp (15 ml) vegetable oil

1 (3" [7.5-cm]) square piece salmon skin

½ (7½ x 8" [19 x 20–cm]) sheet nori

4 oz (115 g) Sushi Rice (page 20)

Sesame seeds

Kaiware (daikon sprouts), cut as close to the root as possible

2 pieces cucumber (see page 51 for cutting technique)

1 piece yamagobo (pickled burdock root)

Bonito flakes

1 tsp wasabi paste, for serving

1 tbsp (15 g) pickled sushi ginger, for serving

1. In a small skillet, heat the vegetable oil over medium heat. Cook the salmon skin for 3 to 4 minutes, or until crispy. Remove from the heat and allow to cool, then cut into strips and set aside.

2. Place the nori on a cutting board, rough side up. Cover the nori with the Sushi Rice according to the directions on page 57 for Uramaki (Rice-Outside Rolls). Sprinkle the sesame seeds on the rice and flip it over. Place the daikon sprouts on the ends of the roll with the leaves hanging out. Place the salmon skin, cucumber and yamagobo on the nori, on top of the daikon sprouts (this will help hold them in place). Roll up the roll according to the directions on page 57, sprinkle with bonito flakes and cover with plastic wrap.

3. Shape the roll with a makisu (bamboo mat). Cut the roll into eight equal pieces. Reshape with the makisu once more. Place the roll on the plate, with the end pieces positioned so the daikon sprouts are standing up. Add the wasabi and pickled sushi ginger to the plate.

CATERPILLAR ROLL

MAKES 1 ROLL

This sushi roll shows the artistic flair of a sushi chef. The avocado must be cut thinly and uniformly so when it is expanded to the side, its subtle transition between green and yellow produces the beautiful effect of a caterpillar. Your knife must be very sharp to achieve this piece of art. In Japanese cuisine, plating is very important; that's why you must be creative and bring not only a flavorful but a visual experience to your guests. You can use other food to make eyes and horns for the caterpillar.

½ avocado, peeled and pitted

1 California Roll (page 61), uncut

Sushi sauce (see page 15)

1 tsp wasabi paste, for serving

1 tbsp (15 g) pickled sushi ginger, for serving

1. On page 52, I showed you my technique for cutting an avocado. For this roll, we are going to cut the avocado into very thin slices instead. Place your avocado half horizontally on a cutting board. Using the tip of your knife, make very thin slices from the top to the bottom. Thin slices will be more flexible when you mold them to the shape of the roll.

2. Using your hand and starting from the bottom of the avocado, push the avocado to flatten it and spread it out. We want to spread the avocado to the same length as the roll. Carefully pick up the avocado with the knife and lay it on top of the California Roll. Place a piece of plastic wrap over the roll and gently mold the avocado to the roll.

3. Using a makisu (bamboo mat), we can firmly shape the roll. Remove the makisu, leaving the plastic wrap in place, and cut into eight equal pieces. Reshape with the makisu and remove the plastic wrap. Decorate the plate with sushi sauce and place the roll on top of the sauce. Add the wasabi and pickled sushi ginger to the plate.

TUNA POKE ROLL

MAKES 1 ROLL

The tuna poke roll is very different from other rolls. When you cut this roll, you plate it differently, so it resembles the shape of a volcano. When you top it with tuna poke, native to Hawaiian cuisine, it looks like a tasty flavor–erupting volcano. This dish is always very impressive, and your guests are going to love it.

---

3 oz (85 g) tuna

1 tbsp (15 ml) soy sauce

1 tbsp (15 ml) sesame oil

1 tsp grated fresh ginger

1 tbsp (15 ml) sriracha (optional, for spicy poke)

2 tbsp (18 g) diced avocado

Wasabi Mayo (page 159), to taste (optional)

Honey Sriracha (page 161), to taste (optional)

4 oz (115 g) Sushi Rice (page 20)

½ (7½ x 8" [19 x 20–cm]) sheet nori

Furikake or sesame seeds

2 pieces cucumber (see page 51 for cutting technique)

2 pieces avocado (see page 52 for cutting technique)

1 stalk asparagus, blanched and cooled

1 jalapeño pepper, sliced, for garnish (optional)

1 tsp wasabi paste, for serving

1 tbsp (15 g) pickled sushi ginger, for serving

1. For this roll, you can use leftover pieces of tuna. Cut your tuna into a small dice (see page 143).

2. Place the tuna in a small bowl. In another bowl, combine the soy sauce, sesame oil, grated ginger and sriracha (if using), and mix well. Gradually add the sauce to the tuna, mixing gently, until it reaches your desired dressed consistency. Any leftover sauce can be stored in the refrigerator for future use. Add the diced avocado to the tuna, as well as some Wasabi Mayo and Honey Sriracha to taste (if using). Store the poke in the refrigerator until you are ready to use it.

3. Spread the rice on the nori according to the directions on page 57 for Uramaki (Rice-Outside Rolls). Sprinkle the furikake or sesame seeds on the rice and flip over. Place the cucumber, avocado and asparagus on the nori and roll up the roll according to the directions on page 57.

4. Place a piece of plastic wrap over the roll and shape with a makisu (bamboo mat). Remove the mat and cut the roll into eight equal pieces. Reshape the roll one more time with your makisu.

5. Place the pieces of the roll on the plate, laying them down on their side. Using a small spoon, place a mound of tuna poke on top of each piece. Place a slice of jalapeño (if using) on top of each roll. Add the wasabi paste and pickled sushi ginger to the plate.

SOY SHEET HEART ROLL

MAKES 2 HEART-SHAPED ROLLS

At my school, the Sushi Chef Institute, I host sushi workshops once a month. These workshops are for people who want to learn sushi in a nonprofessional capacity, and since we usually only have a couple of hours, I like to incorporate unique and fun activities. Most people know rolls, but they don't know that rolls can be shaped into other things. This heart-shaped roll is simple to make but it always makes a good impression. I love to teach this roll to first-time sushi makers since it's a great gift they can make for their loved ones. I hope to see *you* at my school someday so we can make and eat sushi together.

½ (7½ x 8" [19 x 20–cm]) sheet nori

3 oz (85 g) Sushi Rice (page 20)

1 stick imitation crab

1 piece cucumber (see page 51 for cutting technique)

1 piece avocado (see page 52 for cutting technique)

½ (7½ x 8" [19 x 20–cm]) red soy sheet (see page 16)

1 tsp wasabi paste, for serving

1 tbsp (15 g) pickled sushi ginger, for serving

1. Place the nori horizontally on a cutting board. With your knife, cut off one-third of the nori and save for another use.

2. Place the remaining two-thirds of the nori vertically on the board and cover with the Sushi Rice according to the directions on pages 93 and 94.

(continued)

3. Turn over the nori, place the imitation crabmeat, cucumber and avocado in the middle and roll up the roll following the instructions on page 57.

4. Place the red soy sheet over the roll so that only one edge is touching the cutting board.

5. Cover the roll with a makisu (bamboo mat) and press down with your palms while pressing in with your fingers to create a wave shape. From the side, it should look like half of a heart.

6. Cut the excess of the red soy sheet, moisten your knife blade with temizu (see page 44) and swipe the tip of your knife under the roll to separate it from the cutting board.

7. Cut the roll into four equal pieces.

8. Two pieces placed together will form the shape of an entire heart. Put your pieces on your serving plate and add the wasabi and pickled sushi ginger to the plate.

SPRING SUSHI ROLL

MAKES 1 ROLL

Spring rolls are originally from Vietnam. In the United States, it is a popular item that wraps vegetables, cooked seafood or meats in rice paper. In this recipe, Vietnam and Japan come together by bringing sushi ingredients into the filling. This is a nice and healthy appetizer that can be enjoyed the best during summertime.

2 slices (20 g) tuna (cut using the Sogigiri Neta Cut, page 106)

1 sheet edible rice paper (sold packaged for spring rolls)

2 spinach leaves

1 piece cucumber (see page 51 for cutting technique)

1 piece avocado (see page 52 for cutting technique)

Thinly sliced carrot

½ oz (15 g) Sushi Rice (page 20; see note)

1 shrimp (see page 27 for prep technique)

1 tsp wasabi paste, for serving

1 tbsp (15 g) pickled sushi ginger, for serving

Spicy ponzu sauce (start with homemade [page 160] or store-bought ponzu and add a little sriracha), for serving

1. Cut your sliced tuna into thin strips.

2. Wet a lint-free towel and fold it to the size of the rice paper. You will rest the rice paper on the towel while assembling the roll. Dip the rice paper in warm water for 3 seconds. Place the rice paper on the towel. It will become softer as the water is absorbed by the rice paper.

3. The width of your roll will be determined by how you place your ingredients. Leave about an inch (2.5 cm) of space along one side of the paper to make it easier to close the roll. Place your spinach on the lower third of the rice paper. Then, add the cucumber, avocado, carrot and tuna. Add the Sushi Rice on top of the spinach by shaping it into a long strip. Place the shrimp next to the spinach so you will be able to see it after you close the roll.

4. Starting from the bottom, pick up the rice paper and bring it over the fillings. With your left hand, bring the left side up to close one side of the roll. From the bottom, roll it over. Then, with your right hand, bring up the right side, closing the roll completely. Finish rolling the roll over itself. Cut in half on an angle. Transfer to a plate and add the wasabi and pickled sushi ginger to the plate. Serve with spicy ponzu sauce for dipping.

CHEF ANDY'S NOTE: When making this spring roll, it is important to have all your ingredients ready before you start rolling. These rolls can also be made with or without rice.

CHEF ANDY'S SIGNATURE ROLL
(NASU SPECIAL ROLL)

MAKES 1 ROLL

This roll is not so much my "signature" for the roll itself, but because of the sauces it uses, which I created. I really enjoy inventing sauces. Eggplant is one of my favorite vegetables and I wanted to come up with a sauce that paired well with its rich and sweet unique flavor. I love to create fusion recipes with other cuisines, and that is something that I encourage in my school. It shows that sushi is versatile and not just limited to Asian ingredients. I mixed butter with white miso and changed some ingredients from Japanese ones to create a new sauce based on a wine-based butter sauce I learned a long time ago. For me, it's very special when you mix traditional Japanese ingredients, such as white miso and Dashi (page 32), with common ingredients from other cultures, such as capers and butter. Decoration (and flavor) are very important in Japanese culture, so I top my roll with angel hair French fries to add texture and visual appeal. Just with one bite, your mouth will feel all types of flavors and textures and how they complement one another so well. My students also love this roll.

CHEF ANDY'S SIGNATURE ROLL

6 thin slices Japanese eggplant

1 tsp vegetable oil

2 oz (55 g) tuna

3 tbsp (45 ml) Spicy Mayo (page 158)

½ (7½ x 8" [19 x 20–cm]) sheet nori

4 oz (115 g) Sushi Rice (page 20)

2 slices avocado (see page 52 for cutting technique)

1 tsp wasabi paste, for serving

1 tbsp (15 g) pickled sushi ginger, for serving

CHEF ANDY'S SIGNATURE SAUCE

4 tbsp (60 ml) Dashi (page 32)

1 tbsp (16 g) saikyo miso (white sweet miso)

1 tbsp (14 g) unsalted butter

1 tsp capers, drained

GARNISHES

Vegetable oil, for frying

2 oz (55 g) thinly julienned potatoes

Chile threads, for garnish (see note)

(continued)

1. Begin making the signature roll: Slice the eggplant at an angle to make longer thin slices about 1 inch (2.5 cm) wide and 2 inches (5 cm) long. Thin slices will be flexible and will easily cover the roll. In a medium-sized skillet over medium heat, heat the vegetable oil and add the eggplant slices. Grill for 3 to 4 minutes, making sure you flip them and grill both sides. Remove from the heat and set aside to cool. These will go on top of the roll.

2. Prepare the signature sauce: In a small pan, combine the dashi, miso, butter and capers and bring to a boil over medium-high heat, stirring to break up the miso. Lower the heat to a simmer and cook for about 3 minutes, until the butter is melted and the sauce has thickened. Set aside and keep warm.

3. Prepare the garnish: In a medium-sized skillet, heat 1 inch (2.5 cm) of vegetable oil over medium heat. Fry the potatoes at 350°F (180°C) until golden brown. Drain on paper towels and set aside.

4. Return now to preparing the signature roll: For the tuna that goes inside this roll, you can use leftover pieces from making another roll. Chop them into a small dice. Place the tuna in a bowl and gradually add the Spicy Mayo until it reaches your desired level of spiciness. (If you have any spicy tuna leftovers, consume them. I don't recommend storing it for more than 24 hours.)

5. Place the nori on a cutting board, rough side up, and cover with rice according to the directions on page 57 for Uramaki (Rice-Outside Rolls). Flip the nori over and place the spicy tuna in a line down the middle. Place the avocado next to the spicy tuna and roll up the roll according to the directions on page 57.

6. Place the grilled eggplant on top of the roll at an angle, starting from the left. Cover the roll with plastic wrap and shape with a makisu (bamboo mat). Cut into eight equal pieces and place on a plate. Drizzle the sauce over the roll. Top the roll with the fried potatoes and then with the chile threads. Serve immediately. Add the wasabi and pickled sushi ginger to the plate.

CHEF ANDY'S NOTE: I really enjoy using dried red chile threads for decoration, to add a little flavor, heat and color to dishes. They are popular in Asian cuisine. You can find them in most Asian supermarkets.

FUTOMAKI (THICK ROLLS)

Futomaki are impressive rolls with as many as six or seven different ingredients. These rolls are used in Japan for festivities. Because the nori is outside, this is what you will taste first. And since there are so many ingredients inside, you will discover the flavors of the many fillings and have a party in your mouth. These instructions have been written with a right-handed person in mind. If you are left-handed, just mirror the instructions. Whenever handling sushi rice, remember to use temizu (see page 44). Dip your fingers in the temizu whenever you feel the rice is beginning to stick to your hands or is becoming hard to work with. The temperature of your rice should ideally be body temperature, about 98°F (37°C).

HOW TO ROLL FUTOMAKI

1. Place your nori vertically on a makisu (bamboo mat), rough side up. Pick up 5 ounces (140 g) of prepared Sushi Rice (page 20) in your left hand and gently shape it into a log the width of the nori sheet.

2. Place the rice 2 inches (5 cm) from the top of the nori sheet.

3. Place your left hand on the left edge of the nori—this will keep the rice from going off the nori—and, using your thumb on your right hand, push some the rice toward the top left corner of the nori, stopping 1 inch (2.5 cm) from the top.

(continued)

4. Using three fingers of your right hand, pull some rice down to the bottom left side of the nori.

5. Place your right hand on the right edge of the nori and, using the thumb on your left hand, push the rice toward the top right corner of the nori, stopping 1 inch (2.5 cm) from the top.

6. Using the fingers of your left hand, pull the rice down to the bottom right corner of the nori.

7. Place your filling in the center of the rice. If you have multiple ingredients, lay them side by side in a long, thin line spread evenly—go all the way to the edges horizontally, not vertically. You still want space to be able to close the roll.

8. After setting your ingredients side by side, you can stack the remaining ones into a small mountain.

9. Use your thumbs to lift the nori up by 90 degrees. While doing this, use your fingers to hold the fillings tightly in place. With your right hand, roll over the fillings until you meet the rice, then pinch the roll gently.

10. Continue to roll with your fingers and smear a couple of rice grains on the remaining edge of the nori to glue the ends together. Place your makisu on top of the roll and gently press over the roll to shape it.

11. Remove the makisu and now your roll is ready to be cut. Dip the tip of a sharp knife in your temizu and hold the knife upright, allowing the water to run down the length of the blade. Cut the roll into eight equal pieces, wiping your knife on a wet clean towel as needed.

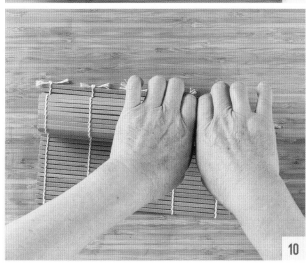

SALMON SUNSET ROLL

MAKES 1 ROLL

When fileting a whole salmon for sushi preparation, the tail area's meat can be a little tough, so I pair slices of it with asparagus, roll them up and then coat the roll with panko and fry it. I recommend you start getting familiar with fish by using precut salmon filets. This roll is also an artistic sushi chef piece. With the help of spicy and sweet Thai sauce and sushi sauce (see page 15), I design a sunset landscape on the plate. I'll help you master this design, too.

3 oz (85 g) salmon

2½ (7½ x 8" [19 x 20–cm]) sheets nori

1 stalk asparagus, blanched and cooled

Neutral oil, for frying

All-purpose flour, for dusting

1 large egg, beaten

½ cup (30 g) panko bread crumbs

3 oz (85 g) Sushi Rice (page 20)

2 tbsp (30 ml) Thai sweet chili sauce (I use Mae Ploy™ brand)

1 tbsp (15 ml) sushi sauce (see page 15)

1 tsp wasabi paste, for serving

1 tbsp (15 g) pickled sushi ginger, for serving

1. For this roll, you can use leftover pieces of fish from making another roll. Cut the salmon into six slices the same width of your nori, using the Sogigiri Neta Cut (page 106).

2. Place one nori sheet vertically on a cutting board. Working lengthwise, cover half of the nori sheet with the sliced salmon. Place the asparagus in the middle of the salmon and roll up the roll according to the directions for futomaki on page 93 (no rice is used at this point). The asparagus tip should be hanging out.

3. In a large, deep pot, heat 1 inch (2.5 cm) of oil over medium-high heat. Place the flour in a shallow bowl, the beaten egg in another bowl and the panko in a third bowl. Dredge the entire roll in the flour, roll in the beaten egg and then roll in the panko. When the oil reaches 350°F (180°C), deep-fry the roll for 2 minutes on each side. Remove the roll from the oil and drain on paper towels.

4. Place the second sheet of nori vertically on the cutting board. Spread with the rice, covering 90 percent of the nori, following the directions on page 93. Place the panko-crusted roll on the rice. Attach the remaining ½ nori sheet lengthwise to the last nori sheet that goes on the outside of the roll with a few pieces of rice to act as the "glue," so you can close and roll up the futomaki roll according to the directions on page 93. Shape with a makisu (bamboo mat) and cut into six equal pieces.

5. On a round plate, drizzle the sweet chili sauce in a circle toward the top of the plate. This will be the sun. Place the sushi sauce in a line under sun. Place the roll on the plate below the sushi sauce. The first piece with the asparagus tip can be positioned so the asparagus is standing up. The remaining pieces can be leaned against the first piece. Add the wasabi and pickled sushi ginger to the plate.

SPIDER ROLL

MAKES 1 ROLL

For this roll, I don't use spiders but soft-shell crab, which is a unique kind of crab. The shell is soft and doesn't need to be removed to cook it. After frying the crab and rolling it up, I like to decorate the plate with a spider net drawn with sushi sauce (see page 15). This is one of my personal favorite rolls because of its crunch and the nuanced flavor of the crab.

---

1 soft-shell crab

2 tbsp (16 g) tempura flour, plus more for dredging

2 tbsp (30 ml) water

Vegetable oil, for frying

½ (7½ x 8" [19 x 20–cm]) sheet nori

3 oz (85 g) Sushi Rice (page 20)

Kaiware (daikon sprouts; optional)

1 piece cucumber (see page 51 for cutting technique)

1 piece avocado (see page 52 for cutting technique)

1 piece yamagobo (pickled burdock root; optional)

1 piece green leaf lettuce

2 tsp (10 g) orange tobiko (flying fish eggs; optional)

6 tbsp (90 ml) sushi sauce (see page 15), for decoration

1 tsp wasabi paste, for serving

1 tbsp (15 g) pickled sushi ginger, for serving

1. Dry the crab with paper towels. In a medium-sized bowl, make the tempura batter by mixing the tempura flour with the water. Dredge the crab with extra flour, shaking off the excess, then dip into the tempura batter. In a medium-sized skillet, heat 1 inch (2.5 cm) of the oil to 350°F (180°C). Fry the crab for 3 to 4 minutes. Drain on paper towels.

2. Place the nori vertically on a cutting board and spread the rice to cover 90 percent of it, according to the directions on page 93. Place the kaiware (if using) on the ends of the rice with the leaves hanging out. Place the cucumber, avocado and yamagobo (if using) on the rice. On top of this, place the lettuce leaf. Spread the tobiko (if using) in a line across the lettuce and place the crab on top. The crab should be in the center of the roll. Don't worry if the legs hang out; this is part of the decoration. Roll up and shape with a makisu (bamboo mat) according to the directions on page 93. Cut the roll into six equal pieces.

3. Using your sushi sauce, draw a spiral on a round plate. Place a skewer or a chopstick in the center of your spiral, and with the tip of your skewer, draw straight lines going from the center outward. This will help you create a "web" pattern of the sauce on your plate. You can make six to eight lines. Place an end piece of the roll flat on the plate with the kaiware and crab standing up. Lean the four inside pieces against the first piece and place the last piece standing up. Add the wasabi and pickled sushi ginger to the plate.

3A

3B

HALLOWEEN SUSHI ROLL

MAKES 1 ROLL

Holidays like Halloween are a great time to get creative. I like to create sushi characters and be very artistic with it. In the United States, Halloween is a big celebration and is loved by both children and adults. This roll has the same purpose. It is meant to be enjoyed by both children and their parents while, at the same time, eating a healthy meal. It is a very fun activity to do with your family and friends. Creating decorative sushi requires a slightly different technique than typical futomaki rolls. We will assemble the components first and then assemble the roll, so we can create the design seen when you cut the roll into pieces. You can find *kamaboko* (fish cake), which is commonly premade, in most Asian supermarkets. Kamaboko is made out of white fish and has a very light fish flavor, slightly similar to shrimp. Let's make something fun with it!

---

2 (7½ x 8" [19 x 20–cm]) sheets nori

1 white kamaboko (steamed fish cake)

3 pieces cucumber (see page 51 for cutting technique)

10 oz (280 g) Sushi Rice (page 20), divided

1 tsp wasabi paste, for serving

1 tbsp (15 g) pickled sushi ginger, for serving

1. Cut 1 sheet of nori in half horizontally, and set one of the halves aside. Cut four ¼-inch (6-mm) strips off the edge of the other ½ sheet.

2. Place the kamaboko, flat side down, on a cutting board and make four cuts lengthwise about halfway through but without cutting all the way through, to keep the kamaboko intact. Insert the ¼-inch (6-mm) nori strips into the cuts. These will be the teeth of our design. Set aside.

(continued)

3. Cut three more thin strips from the nori we used to make the teeth. Wrap each piece of cucumber with a strip of nori and secure it by crushing a grain of rice on the edge. This will act as the "glue." Place these seam side down and set aside.

4. Place the uncut ½ sheet of nori on the cutting board and attach the reserved ½ sheet to it with several grains of rice. You now have a sheet that is 150 percent longer than normal.

5. Place 4 ounces (115 g) of the Sushi Rice in the center of the long sheet of nori and spread it—the nori should be horizontal and the rice should be spread horizontally—leaving 1 inch (2.5 cm) uncovered on opposite ends of the sheet (see the directions for spreading rice on futomaki on page 93).

6. Place 2 ounces (55 g) of the Sushi Rice in the middle of the nori and form it into a triangular shape. Lay one piece of nori-wrapped cucumber on both sides of the triangle. These are the eyes.

7. Spread 2 ounces (55 g) of the Sushi Rice on top of the eyes to secure them in place, creating a thin layer on top. Place the third piece of nori-wrapped cucumber in the center of this layer of rice and cover with the remaining 2 ounces (55 g) of Sushi Rice. This will be the nose of our design.

8. Place the kamaboko (fish cake), flat side down, on top of the nose.

9. Roll up the roll according to the directions on page 93 and shape gently with a makisu (bamboo mat).

10. Cut into four equal pieces and reveal the face of your Halloween-themed design. Put your pieces on a serving plate and add the wasabi and pickled sushi ginger to the plate.

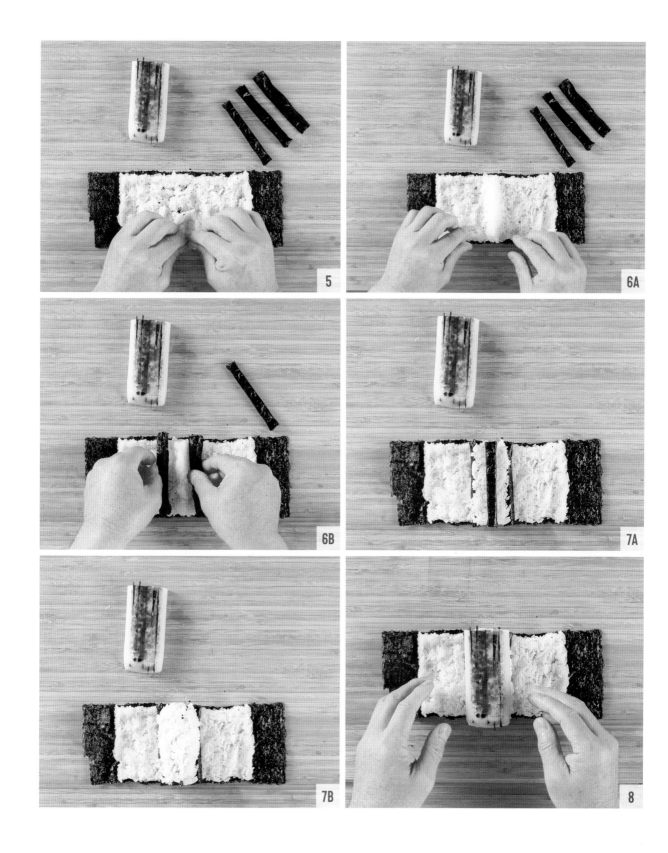

NIGIRI

Nigiri sushi is a style that most people perceive as high-end and more traditional. Originally, nigiri was street food during the Edo period in Japan about 200 years ago. *Nigiri* literally translates to "two hands to make rice ball food."

I learned how to make nigiri when I was 18 years old, back in Japan. After my master taught me, I remember always practicing the steps for shaping nigiri rice with a little piece of wrapped daikon that resembled the final shape of a piece of nigiri. I think that I've made more than 2 million pieces of nigiri so far and used about 200 or more kinds of fish, including the delicate and dangerous blowfish. Most people's favorite nigiri are the ones made with tuna—I am no exception, as you may have noticed. I especially love the toro (fatty underbelly). I love the harmony among well-seasoned sushi rice, the wasabi under the fresh tuna on top and a little soy sauce.

Mastering the first, foundational steps are the most important when it comes to making nigiri. For my students at the Sushi Chef Institute, the first week is key. The hardest part is always dealing with the sushi rice, so it doesn't stick everywhere. You want it to hold together and not fall apart when you pick it up with your chopsticks. You should aim for beauty when making your nigiri—make sure it looks sexy. One of the biggest differences between Japanese and foreign sushi is the freshness of the fish, the seasonality of the ingredients and how elegant it looks. We'll work on mastering that defined nigiri look and shape in the pages ahead.

Nigiri is particularly known in *omakase* at sushi bars. This means "leave it to the chef." If you want to have a deeper look into this style and what the life of a master sushi chef is like, watch the 2011 film *Jiro Dreams of Sushi* by director David Gelb. This movie portrayed a radical view of sushi bars and a sushi chef's image.

Japanese people love fish and consume it in large quantities, and they prefer nigiri sushi over rolls. I personally prefer nigiri as well. When we consume fish in Japan, we look at it as supporting the fishermen. It is important that you understand where your fish comes from and how it was caught. We need to consume fish acquired through sustainable practices so we can help Mother Nature and our oceans stay healthy and peaceful. We need to think of the following generations after us. Refer to my Tips on Buying Fish and Seafood (page 26) to read more about this.

In this chapter, you will learn the basics of making nigiri so you can start your own omakase with friends and family at home. I will start by showing you the classic cut sushi chefs use for cutting fish for nigiri. I will then walk you through how to make the most popular nigiri, with my own creative recipes for enhancing each one and making it slightly new and different.

CUTTING FISH FOR NIGIRI:
THE SOGIGIRI NETA CUT

When cutting fish for nigiri, it's ideal to start with a block about as wide as the palm of your hand. Fish for nigiri sushi will be approximately 1 inch (2.5 cm) wide, 2 inches (5 cm) long and ¼ inch (6 mm) thick. There is some variation in how thick we cut our fish slices, depending on the type of fish. For instance, white fish should be cut slightly thinner due to the flesh's chewy nature. For white fish, we scale down to about a $^1/_8$-inch (3-mm)-thick slice. As we move through the different recipes for fish and seafood nigiri, I will alert you to any differences in the cutting style. Mostly, though, the following cutting technique is how a majority of fish for nigiri is cut. If you master this technique, you will be well on your way to making a delicious and visually stunning arrangement of nigiri.

Let's get to it!

1. Place your filet at a 45-degree angle on a cutting board.

2. Remove a triangular-shaped piece from the end of the filet closest to you. Save this piece to use for rolls with a dice cut, such as Tuna Poke Roll (page 83). This cut will give you an angle to easily cut your pieces.

3. Next, we will position the edge of the knife (the heel of it) on the fish and follow the angle we just created. Place your two fingers on the end of your fish to help guide your slice.

4. Slice a piece of fish that is 1 inch (2.5 cm) wide, 2 inches (5 cm) long and ¼ inch (6 mm) thick, following the angle of the fish with your knife.

5. Now, your slices are ready to be assembled into a nigiri (see page 108).

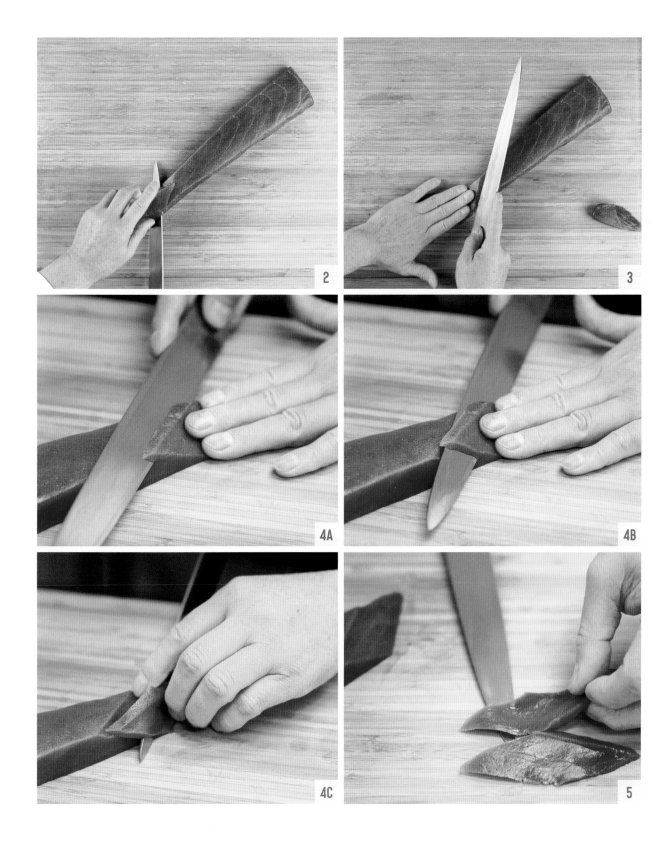

1A

1B

1C

MAKING CLASSIC NIGIRI

Nigiri sushi is also known as Edomae sushi (Edo is the old name of Tokyo). Sushi chefs used to only use seafood from Tokyo's bay to make nigiri sushi. Quick and easy to make, this handcrafted sushi was known as "Edomae nigiri." Although it looks easy to do, it actually takes a chef years to master the technique of forming the rice and properly placing the fish on top. Nigiri sushi should be just large enough to eat in one bite. The rice should separate as you close your mouth. The key point to remember when making nigiri is to form it gently. You can use the following steps to make basic nigiri with any kind of fish or seafood. These instructions have been written with a right-handed person in mind. If you are left-handed, just mirror the instructions.

¾ oz (23 g) Sushi Rice (page 20)

Sliced fish (see page 106 for slicing technique)

Wasabi paste (optional)

1. Pick up the Sushi Rice in your right hand and gently press into the shape of an egg. You can do this by delicately squishing the sides together with your thumb and middle finger, then using two fingers to even out the top. You can also ball up the sushi rice in your fist as you press down on the top, to better shape it.

2. With your left hand, pick up your fish and allow it to rest where your fingers meet your palm.

3. Using your index finger, pick up a small dab of wasabi (if using) and place it on the center of the slice of fish.

4. Place the rice on top of the wasabi.

(continued)

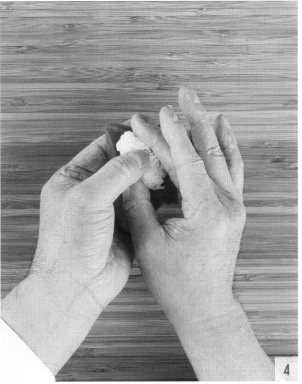

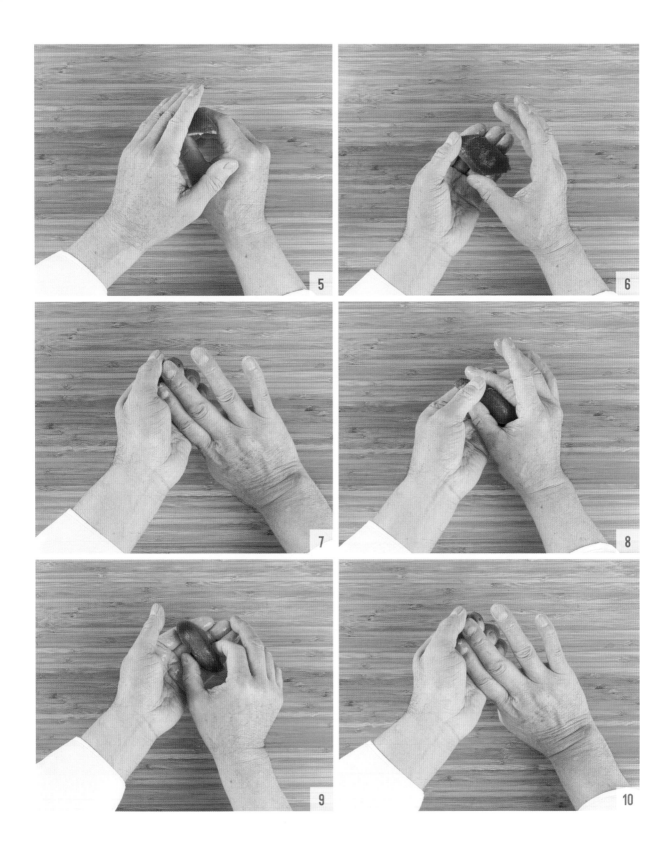

5. Flip the sushi over 180 degrees so the fish is now on top.

6. Place the nigiri back in your left hand where your fingers meet the palm of your hand.

7. Close the fingers of your left hand, cradling the nigiri and with your right hand, gently press down using your index and middle finger.

8. Open your left hand and gently pinch the sides with your thumb and middle finger.

9. Rotate the sushi 180 degrees clockwise.

10. Close your fingers cradling the nigiri and gently press down with your index and middle fingers.

11. Open your hand and gently pinch the sides again with your thumb and middle finger.

12. The finished sushi will look like a boat.

MAGURO (TUNA)

MAKES 2 NIGIRI

Tuna nigiri is an all-time favorite for most sushi lovers, including me. In addition to showing you how to make classic tuna nigiri, I will also show you how to make an alternative for this nigiri by using the Zuke technique, in which you marinate the fish slices. This nigiri is an old-style one. In my opinion, the combination of soy sauce with tuna is a fantastic combination that makes this nigiri's flavor like no other sushi's. Zuke is a great upgrade for the traditional simple nigiri.

Most of the time, you can find frozen tuna *saku* (blocks) that have already been fileted and prepped. If you are using one of those, defrost it slowly by leaving it in your fridge overnight. After defrosting it the first time, you can put it back in your fridge for up to 2 days. To minimize the discoloration of your tuna when storing it in your fridge, wrap it in paper towels and then plastic wrap it. This absorbs the excess of moisture and prevents the air from discoloring the fish. Once you are ready to start, pat dry your filet with paper towels.

2 slices tuna (see page 106 for performing the Sogigiri Neta Cut)

1½ oz (42 g) Sushi Rice (page 20)

Wasabi paste

Pickled sushi ginger, for serving

¼ cup (60 ml) soy sauce (if using Chef Andy's Favorite method)

CLASSIC NIGIRI

1. To make a classic tuna nigiri, assemble two pieces of nigiri following the directions on page 108. Serve with extra wasabi and pickled sushi ginger on the plate.

(continued)

CHEF ANDY'S FAVORITE

1. Pour the soy sauce into a bowl. Place the tuna slices next to each other in the bowl and allow them to marinate for 30 seconds.

2. Flip them over and allow them to marinate for another 30 seconds. The soy sauce will quickly penetrate the fish; the marinating time varies depending on the flavor you are trying to achieve. For this instance, I want a mild and balanced flavor between the saltiness of the soy sauce and the tender, rich flavor of the tuna.

3. Remove the slices from the soy sauce and place them on a paper towel to drain the excess soy sauce from the tuna. You want to pat dry the top of the slices as well.

4. Assemble your nigiri following the steps on page 108. Put your pieces on a serving plate and add the wasabi and pickled sushi ginger to the plate.

SHAKE (SALMON)

MAKES 2 NIGIRI

Salmon is another fish that cannot be left out of the sushi menu. The soft yet rich texture and flavor of salmon makes it very versatile when pairing it with other ingredients and techniques. This has made salmon nigiri a signature item at most sushi bars. One of my alternatives for this popular sushi is to add an avocado slice on top with a little piece of lemon when served raw, but in this recipe, I will show you an alternative perfect for those who can't or won't eat raw fish. Avocado's buttery texture and natural flavor makes this a beautiful collaboration. For salmon, we will also use the Sogigiri Neta Cut, but I like to do it slightly differently for this particular fish. I think it makes it easier. Make sure to pay attention to the following directions.

Salmon can be found in blocks that have been prepped for sushi at most Asian supermarkets. You shouldn't consume sushi made from regular salmon filets. Salmon carries a bacteria called *Anisakis*; that's why salmon for sushi must be salted and frozen for at least one week before being safe to eat raw. You can always ask your supermarket fish specialist for details about the grade of your fish, and whether it's safe for sushi and sashimi. If your filet is frozen, you want to defrost it slowly by leaving it in your fridge overnight. After defrosting it the first time, you can put it back in your fridge for up to 2 days. When storing it in your fridge, plastic wrap it tightly. Once you are ready to start, pat dry your filet with paper towels.

2 pieces salmon (see below for cutting technique)

1½ oz (42 g) Sushi Rice (page 20)

Wasabi paste

Pickled sushi ginger, for serving

Soy sauce, for brushing (optional)

(continued)

4A

4B

4C

CLASSIC NIGIRI

1. To make a classic salmon nigiri, place your salmon filet horizontally on a cutting board so the center line (usually a very white visible line) of the filet is parallel to the cutting board's lower edge.

2. Vertically cut the salmon filet into a block approximately 2½ inches (6.5 cm) wide. Place the block you just cut horizontally on the cutting board.

3. Your goal is to obtain a slice that is 1 inch (2.5 cm) wide and ¼ inch (6 mm) thick. The length is already determined by the width of your filet.

4. To perform the cut, position the edge of the knife (the heel) on the fish and slice all the way through with your whole blade. Most of the time, your salmon filets will have the skin on. After performing your cut and reaching the salmon skin, make a cut parallel to the cutting board to separate the slice from the skin. Now, your slices are ready to be assembled in a nigiri following the directions on page 108.

CHEF ANDY'S NOTE: Salmon filets are thinner on the edges and gradually get thicker toward the center. This is what is going to determine your cutting angles. You will have to adjust your angles depending on the filet you are able to purchase. As you cut closer to the center of the filet, your cuts will straighten up. Usually, for your first slice, your knife could be almost flat (parallel to your cutting board). As you cut toward the center, the angle of the knife will get higher and higher until it becomes 90 degrees.

5

6

CHEF ANDY'S FAVORITE

1. Cut some slices from your filet by following the Sogigiri Neta Cut instructions (page 106) for salmon within the classic nigiri recipe to the left.

2. Make four to six parallel small cuts diagonal to the width of the slice of fish, but do not cut all the way through the fish. Do this throughout the whole slice of each piece. This will not only enhance the presentation of your nigiri, but will allow the sauce we will pair it with to penetrate deeper into the fish.

3. Rotate the slice of fish 90 degrees and make four to six more cuts, not too deep, making sure not to cut all the way through the fish, throughout the slice, so as to create a grid pattern.

4. Assemble your nigiri following the steps on page 108.

5. Place your nigiri on a fire-resistant plate and sear lightly with a kitchen torch for about 10 seconds. Timing is subjective; sear for a shorter or longer period according to your liking of cooked to raw fish. Creating a grid pattern allows the flame from the torch to penetrate deeper into the fish, melting more of the fat and increasing the umami of your nigiri. Just make sure you don't burn your fish. If you don't have a torch, you might be tempted to use a broiler, but this won't have the same effect and will dry up your rice.

6. Put your pieces on your serving plate and add wasabi and pickled sushi ginger to the plate. You can brush a little soy sauce on top of your nigiri to enhance your experience.

EBI (SHRIMP)

MAKES 2 NIGIRI

Shrimp nigiri is an item that cannot be missed on the sushi roster. This is one of the very few nigiri that is cooked and marinated. Also, there are more steps in its preparation than other nigiri sushi, so make sure to read the following directions carefully. As a variation for this nigiri, I like to pair it with tobiko. Tobiko is small flying fish roe that adds a nice crunch and saltiness when you bite into it. Orange tobiko complements beautifully with shrimp's white and orange color and the texture of both together is something that I enjoy very much.

2 shrimp

1½ oz (42 g) Sushi Rice (page 20)

Wasabi paste

½ (7½ x 8" [19 x 20–cm]) sheet nori (if using Chef Andy's Favorite method)

½ oz (15 g) orange tobiko, for garnish (if using Chef Andy's Favorite method; optional)

Pickled sushi ginger, for serving

CLASSIC NIGIRI

1. To make a classic ebi nigiri, prepare your shrimp following the prep instructions on page 27. Then, assemble your nigiri following the directions on page 108.

CHEF ANDY'S FAVORITE

1. I really enjoy the flavor of shrimp nigiri as is, but I like to upscale its presentation and texture. First, assemble the rice for your nigiri following the steps on page 108.

2. Lay ½ sheet of nori horizontally on your cutting board. We are going to cut strips from the right edge that are ¼ inch (6 mm) wide; the length is determined by that of the half sheet of nori.

3. Add a small amount of wasabi to the underside of your shrimp. On top of this, add half of the tobiko (if using) to each piece of shrimp.

4. Finish forming your shrimp nigiri according to the directions on page 108. Wrap each nigiri piece with one of your nori strips by placing the strip on the center of your nigiri and wrapping the edges underneath with your thumb and middle finger.

5. Flip over the nigiri and bring the two ends of the strip together one over the other. Then, place your nigiri on the cutting board and the moisture will seal the nori.

6. Put your pieces on a serving plate and add wasabi and pickled sushi ginger to the plate.

HAMACHI (YELLOWTAIL)

MAKES 2 NIGIRI

This kind of nigiri is craved by more experienced sushi lovers—another must at most sushi bars. Yellowtail is a delicacy that, if it's served fresh, its fishiness won't bother you. I like to use the *Yakishimo* (sear-by-fire) technique for a variation of this classic nigiri, which I show you how to do in the following recipe. This technique takes away some of that fishiness that yellowtail has. I top this variation recipe with *yuzu-kosho*, which is a special sauce of yuzu (a fruit that is a cross between a wild citrus and sour mandarin) and chile pepper. This is commonly bought premade, and you can find it mostly at Asian super-markets or online. You want to look for the semiliquid sauce version of it, not the paste. It should come in a tall sauce bottle like table soy sauce. All the flavors in this dish create a harmonious balance that anybody can enjoy.

---

2 pieces yellowtail (see below for cutting technique)

1½ oz (42 g) Sushi Rice (page 20)

1 tbsp (15 ml) yuzu-kosho

Wasabi paste

Pickled sushi ginger, for serving

CLASSIC NIGIRI

1. For yellowtail, you must trim away any dark red portions (the bloodline, which you will find on the border of the thicker side of the filet) so only the pink flesh remains. The bloodline is usually very fishy and will give you an unpleasant metallic taste; that's the reason we must remove it before performing the Sogigiri Neta Cut. After this, place the filet at a 45-degree angle on the cutting board. To make a classic yellowtail nigiri, perform the Sogigiri Neta Cut (page 106) on your filet and then assemble your nigiri following the directions on page 108.

CHEF ANDY'S FAVORITE

1. Cut your yellowtail filet by following the classic nigiri trimming and cutting instructions.

2. Next, make parallel small cuts along the length of the slice of fish, throughout the whole slice, making sure not to cut all the way through the fish so the slice stays intact. This will not only enhance the presentation of your nigiri but will allow the sauce we will pair it with to penetrate deeper into the fish.

3. Rotate the slice of fish 90 degrees and make small cuts lengthwise in the opposite direction, to create a grid pattern. Again, make sure not to cut too deep so the slice stays intact.

4. Assemble your nigiri following the steps on page 108.

5. Place your nigiri on a fire-resistant plate and sear lightly with a kitchen torch for about 10 seconds. Timing is subjective; sear for a shorter or longer period according to your liking of raw to cooked fish. Creating a grid pattern allows the flame from the torch to penetrate deeper into the fish, melting more of the fat and increasing the umami of your nigiri. Just make sure you don't burn your fish. If you don't have a torch, you might be tempted to use a broiler, but this won't have the same effect and will dry up your rice.

6. To finish, carefully pour a few drops of yuzu-kosho on top. Don't add more than this; too much will overpower the fish and your experience won't be as authentic.

7. Serve your nigiri pieces with wasabi and pickled sushi ginger.

TAI (RED SNAPPER)

MAKES 2 NIGIRI

Red snapper is known for its lean white meat. It contains vitamin A and plenty of omega-3 fatty acids. Its sweet and soft taste makes it very enjoyable when eaten on nigiri. For the variation of the classic recipe, I like to use the Yakishimo technique, which consists of torching the skin and searing the meat. The nice burnt flavor stimulates your appetite and pairs wonderfully with the natural sweetness of this fish. Red snapper needs to be sliced thinly to be fully appreciated as it is very chewy. This is a characteristic of white-fleshed fish. The following instructions have been written for a right-handed person. If you are left-handed, simply mirror the instructions.

---

2 slices red snapper (see below for cutting technique)

1½ oz (42 g) Sushi Rice (page 20)

Wasabi paste

Pickled sushi ginger, for serving

CLASSIC NIGIRI

1. For red snapper, we will use the Sogigiri Neta Cut (page 106). If you have cut your own whole red snapper (see my tutorial on page 35), congratulations! But before performing the Sogigiri Neta Cut, you will want to remove the skin if making a classic red snapper nigiri. To remove the skin, place the filet, skin side down, horizontally on a cutting board, on the edge of the board closest to you. The widest part of the filet should be pointed to the right. Holding the filet with your left index and middle finger, make a small vertical incision down to the skin about a ¼ inch (6 mm) from the edge of the filet. Holding your knife at a 10-degree angle (almost flat) with your right hand while you hold the edge of the fish with your left hand, slide the knife in a sawing motion toward the other end of the filet. You can throw away the skin. To cut your nigiri slices, place your filet at a 45-degree angle on the cutting board and perform the Sogigiri Neta Cut (page 106). Assemble your nigiri following the directions on page 108.

CHEF ANDY'S FAVORITE

1. For this variation, I will use the Yakishimo technique, which is used if you want to keep the skin on your filet. Place your filet on a fire-resistant plate or tray. Do not cut it into pieces at this point. Fill a bowl with ice water and keep it close by.

2. Lightly sear the top of the fish with a kitchen torch until the skin is nicely golden brown. You can use the torch for about 10 seconds throughout the filet. Timing is subjective, but I recommend searing this fish's skin for this amount of time, since it can be really chewy. Just make sure you don't burn your fish—move your torch throughout the filet's skin so it sears evenly. If you don't have a torch, you might be tempted to use a broiler, but this won't have the same effect and your fish will be cooked instead of torched. We are searing only the skin, not the whole filet.

3. Place your seared filet in the ice water and let sit for about 2 minutes to stop the cooking.

4. Place a paper towel or clean kitchen towel on a cutting board and remove the filet from the ice water. Pat the filet dry, then place it at a 45-dregree angle on your cutting board, skin side down.

5. Cut two slices from your filet, using the Sogigiri Neta Cut (page 106), and assemble your nigiri following the instructions on page 108.

6. Put your pieces on a serving plate and add wasabi and pickled sushi ginger to the plate.

UNI (SEA URCHIN)

MAKES 2 NIGIRI

Uni has become the most popular item at high-end sushi bars. Its creamy texture and sweet flavor has made it an item that all sushi lovers crave when going to a sushi bar. Sea urchin is mostly served *gunkan* style, which we will practice in my recipe variation. Sea urchin has very little fat, and due to its diet of mostly kelp, it provides good quantities of protein, omega-3 fatty acids and dietary fiber. It also contains vitamins and minerals that can be found in greens and legumes. Sea urchin can be found in specialized Asian seafood markets, prepackaged. It's usually sold individually in trays. Be gentle when handling sea urchin, as it is very delicate and soft and can fall apart easily. I recommend buying fresh sea urchin if you are using it for sushi. Frozen sea urchin is better for cooked items.

The gunkan style used in this recipe was developed so runnier ingredients could be served with sushi. At the Kyūbey sushi restaurant in Ginza, Chef Imada created this style after trying to serve sea urchin or salmon eggs. Due to their nature, these ingredients were difficult to place on top of sushi, so he wrapped nori around a ball of rice, creating a little container. Nigiri sushi is known for having the shape of a boat. *Gunkan* means "warship," so maybe the name has something to do with that relationship. This style opened the possibilities for new ways to enjoy sushi. I think it was an innovative idea. This style of sushi can also be used to hold spicy tuna and makes a great appetizer.

1½ oz (42 g) Sushi Rice (page 20)

2 pieces sea urchin

½ (7½ x 8" [19 x 20–cm]) sheet nori

1 small cucumber (if using Chef Andy's Favorite; optional)

2 quail eggs (if using Chef Andy's Favorite method)

Wasabi paste, for serving

Pickled sushi ginger, for serving

CLASSIC NIGIRI

1. Because sea urchin is so soft, we will make these nigiri in a different way. Divide your rice into two equal balls and gently form them into boat shapes as shown on page 108. Place them horizontally on the cutting board. Carefully pick up the sea urchin and lay one piece on each rice ball. To pick up the sea urchin, you want to have something thin that would slide under it, so you don't break it. I recommend using very thin chopsticks or a small spatula, but you can also carefully use a spoon. Place a small amount of wasabi on top for garnish, if desired.

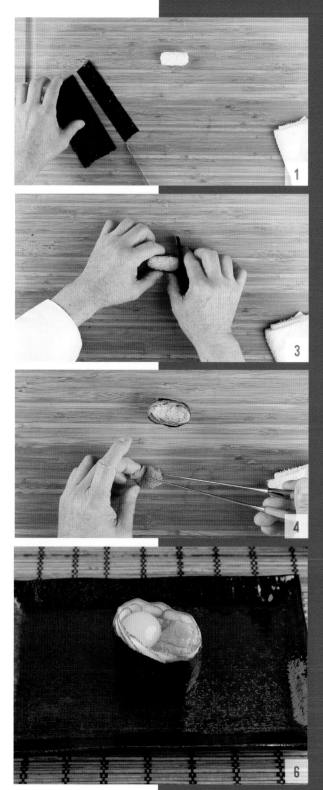

CHEF ANDY'S FAVORITE: GUNKAN STYLE

1. Lay the nori horizontally on a cutting board and cut 1 inch (2.5 cm) off the right side. Turn 90 degrees and cut it into three equal pieces, cutting vertically along the sheet. They should be about 1 inch (2.5 cm) wide and 6 inches (15 cm) long. Save the other piece of nori for more gunkan!

2. Moisten your hands with temizu (see page 44) and pick up ¾ ounce (21 g) of the rice. Gently shape into nigiri following the instructions on page 108, and place it on your cutting board.

3. Dry your hands and pick up your strip of nori. Starting in the middle of your nori strip, wrap the nori around the rice with the rough side touching the rice. Close one end first by pushing the nori against the rice. Take one grain of rice and press it into the remaining edge of the nori strip. This is your "glue" that will keep the gunkan closed. Finish wrapping the nori and gently press the nori to close it.

4. If you would like to upscale your uni gunkan, you can add cucumber as decoration, but this part is optional. Cut a small cucumber in half lengthwise, then cut one of the halves into very thin slices; almost paper thin. Place one slice over the other, creating a little fence and set it inside your nigiri before adding the sea urchin.

5. Place one piece of uni on top of the rice inside of your gunkan. Crack a quail egg and place it on top of the sea urchin. Repeat the previous steps to make the second gunkan.

6. Put your pieces on your serving plate and add wasabi and pickled sushi ginger to the plate. Serve immediately.

HIRAME (HALIBUT)

MAKES 2 NIGIRI AND 5 TABLESPOONS (75 G) MOMIJI-OROSHI

Halibut is very popular among sushi lovers because of its mild and sweet taste. Its flavor is not as fishy as other kinds of fish and its texture is thicker and firmer. Halibut's characteristics make it very suitable for pairing with strong sauces or garnishes. Halibut is a flat fish with eyes on the left. When buying filets, ask that the *engawa* (edges) not be removed, as these are considered a delicacy. Engawa is fin meat that is slightly crunchy and chewy, and it will be on the very edge of the filet. It's considered the best part of halibut. It needs to be sliced thinly to be fully appreciated, as it is very chewy. You can find fresh halibut in Asian supermarkets. Frozen halibut filets are also available. Halibut is better for sushi when it is fresh, but if you purchase frozen, you want to defrost it slowly by leaving it in your fridge overnight. After defrosting it the first time, you can put it back in your fridge for up to 2 days. To store in the refrigerator, plastic wrap it. Once you are ready to start, pat dry your filet with paper towels.

The *yakumi* (condiments) we mainly use for halibut are *momiji-oroshi* (grated daikon with crushed chile pepper) and *sarashi negi* (washed green onions). Washed green onions are used as garnish and an addition to dipping sauces. Washing the onions removes the spiciness and makes them milder. Save the rubber band that comes with the onions when you buy them from the store, as we will use this to hold them in place when we slice them. The crushed chile pepper we use is called *ichimi togarashi*, which is one specific kind of Japanese ground red chile pepper.

YAKUMI

1 (1" [2.5-cm]) piece daikon, peeled

1 tbsp (15 g) ichimi togarashi

5 green onions

NIGIRI

⅓ oz (12 g) halibut (see page 106 for performing the Sogigiri Neta Cut)

1½ oz (42 g) Sushi Rice (page 20)

1 tbsp (15 ml) Ponzu (page 160)

Wasabi paste, for serving

Pickled sushi ginger, for serving

CLASSIC NIGIRI

1. Assemble your nigiri following the directions on page 108.

CHEF ANDY'S FAVORITE

YAKUMI

1. To make momiji-oroshi, grate the piece of peeled daikon very finely by using a rasp grater. Place the grated daikon in a mesh strainer and allow it to drain for 5 minutes. Place 4 tablespoons (60 g) of the drained daikon in a bowl and gradually add ichimi togarashi until you have a nice red color. You can store momiji-oroshi in a sealed container up to 3 days in your refrigerator.

2. To make sarashi negi, wrap the rubber band the green onions came with around the green onions about 2 inches (5 cm) from one end. We will start slicing at this end. Place your onions horizontally on a cutting board and carefully slice them into rounds as thinly as possible. As you approach the rubber band, roll it farther down the onion until you get to the end. Place the green onions on a piece of cheesecloth. Gather the ends of the cheesecloth and twist it closed. Place the parcel under running water, while squeezing out the gooey liquid. When no more gooey liquid comes out, the onions are considered washed and will be much milder.

Now, let's make sushi!

NIGIRI

3. Assemble your halibut nigiri according to the directions on page 108 and lightly brush the nigiri with ponzu. Then, lightly garnish with momiji-oroshi and top it with some sarashi negi. White fish pairs beautifully with citrusy sauces. This version of halibut nigiri will take you to Japan in one bite. It contains a fusion of ingredients and sauces that are part of the base of Japanese cooking. Put your pieces on a serving plate and add wasabi and pickled sushi ginger to the plate.

VEGETARIAN/VEGAN NIGIRI

MAKES 8 NIGIRI

Some people have dietary restrictions. Some others decide to follow a different gastronomic path. Vegetables are known for having wonderful health properties that are very beneficial for our body. In this recipe, I will show you some vegetarian variations of nigiri with some of my favorite vegetables, such as shiitake, which is widely used in Japanese cuisine; asparagus, which is a good source of fiber; and my very favorite vegetable, eggplant. In this recipe, we will be making an ensemble of eight different pieces served all together.

½ (7½ x 8" [19 x 20–cm]) sheet nori

6 oz (170 g) Sushi Rice (page 20)

1 shiitake mushroom, grilled

1 stalk asparagus, blanched and cut in half

1 piece Asian eggplant, sliced at an angle and grilled

1 piece orange bell pepper, grilled

1 piece red bell pepper, grilled

1 small bunch daikon sprouts, blanched

1 red radish, cut into thin rounds

1 piece zucchini, sliced at an angle and grilled

Wasabi paste, for serving

Pickled ginger, for serving

1. Make the nori bands: Lay the nori horizontally on a cutting board. We are going to cut ¼-inch (6-mm)-wide strips from the right edge; your length is determined by the half sheet of nori. Make three strips and set aside.

2. Take ¾ ounce (21 g) of the Sushi Rice and form it into a nigiri shape, according to the directions on page 108. Place it on the cutting board and repeat with the remaining rice until you have eight equal-sized rice balls.

3. Place the shiitake mushroom on top of one ball of rice. Pick up a nori band and wrap it around the nigiri so that the two ends meet at the bottom of the rice. The nori band will hold the shiitake in place and the moisture from the rice will seal the two ends of the nori together. Repeat with the remaining vegetables, one kind of vegetable per rice ball. Wrap nori bands around the asparagus and daikon sprouts nigiri. Place on a plate and add wasabi and pickled sushi ginger to the plate.

OTHER SUSHI STYLES

As I mentioned earlier, each region in Japan has local ingredients or seafood. Each region would only serve sushi on special occasions. This created great food memories in that region's children. Even today, people remember and are very proud of their regional dishes and enjoy trying traditional dishes from other places. The traditional sushi styles have not changed much in the last 200 years in Japan. In Japanese culture, the image of traditional food has not changed at all and remains very strong. It is passed on throughout generations. Some of the sushi styles included in this chapter have become very popular and well known worldwide; others, however, are mostly famous among Japanese people. Some of these special sushi styles are not served by many restaurants.

My favorite special sushi style is *battera* (pressed) sushi made with marinated saba (mackerel) with sushi rice. It is very historical and uses a unique technique to make it. I recently have become keen toward traditional Japanese ways of food and history. They are healthier and I feel that I can travel back in time and imagine what the food and customs were back then. Battera sushi is not very popular overseas, but it is a staple in Japanese culture. I used to make Inari Sushi (page 131) for my daughter while she was growing up. It was easy, simple and very tasty. She loved it. The sweetness of the fried tofu balances the sushi rice flavor and it makes it a great introduction to sushi. It encourages children to develop an interest in other sushi styles, too. In Japan, inari sushi is very popular and we grow up snacking on it. I wanted to pass this culinary tradition to her. In this chapter, I will take you through other very special sushi, such as Temari (page 134), Chirashi (page 136), Temaki (page 133) and Inari (page 131). I want to teach you about some special Japanese countryside techniques and bring you to a side of Japan that not many people know.

INARI SUSHI

MAKES 3 PIECES

Inari is a god and the protector of rice cultivation who lives in many locations in Japan. Inari used to ride a fox that loved fried tofu; that's where the name for this sushi comes from. Inari is fried tofu that has been marinated in soy and sugar and formed into a pouch to contain sushi rice; it looks like a rice container from the old ages. It is one of the first casual foods in eighteenth-century Edo, very inexpensive but delicious. It is great for lunch boxes, and you can keep it longer than other kinds of sushi. It is originally from Tokyo or Nagoya in locations where there are Inari shrines. Inari is available in most Japanese grocery stores. It can be frozen for long-term storage and defrosted as needed.

3 oz (85 g) Sushi Rice (page 20)

White sesame seeds

Black sesame seeds

3 pieces aged inari

1 large egg, scrambled

1. Divide the rice equally among three bowls. In one bowl, mix in some white sesame seeds. In the second bowl, mix in black sesame seeds. The third bowl will be left plain. Open the first inari and insert the rice with the white sesame seeds. Close the flaps and turn over. Fill the next inari with the rice with the black sesame seeds. Close the flaps and turn over. Open the final inari and fill with plain rice. Place that on your plate, rice side up, and put the scrambled egg on top of the rice. Now, you have a trio of inari sushi.

TEMAKI SUSHI (HAND ROLLS)

MAKES 1 HAND ROLL

This eighteenth-century Edo sushi was popular because the people in Edo were very busy and sometimes didn't have too much time, and sushi was eaten by hand, which with the sticky sushi rice wasn't very practical. Chefs started to wrap nori around sushi so it was easy to pick up and eat. The name *temaki* literally means "roll in hand." I really like the idea behind this item. It's quick, easy and anyone can make it and eat it. You don't really need professional skills, and it's great for parties; the prep time is very short, too. In Japan, this is mostly the last item served after eating a sushi course. There are two ways of rolling hand rolls: the cone and the roll. We will go over both in this recipe.

½ oz (15 g) tuna (see page 106 for cutting technique)

½ (7½ x 8" [19 x 20–cm]) sheet nori

1 oz (28 g) Sushi Rice (page 20)

1 piece avocado (see page 52 for cutting technique)

1 piece cucumber (see page 51 for cutting technique)

1. Cut your tuna into two slices, using the Sogigiri Neta Cut (page 106), then cut both slices in half lengthwise.

2. Hold the nori in your hand vertically. Starting in the left corner, place your rice diagonally, spreading it to the bottom of the nori until flattened, similar to when we spread the rice for sushi rolls (see page 45 for more information). Lay the tuna, avocado and cucumber on top of the rice. Take the bottom left corner of the nori and bring it up over the fillings until it meets the top of the nori. This is the start of the cone. Continue to roll until the cone is complete. Use a grain of rice to keep it closed. Eat immediately.

3. The other method to make temaki is a simple roll. Lay the nori vertically on a cutting board. Place the rice across the nori in a line. Place the other ingredients next to the rice and simply roll it up across.

CHEF ANDY'S NOTES: Crispy nori is essential for hand rolls. If you feel the nori is not crispy, you can reheat it in a toaster oven for a few seconds to make it crispy again.

This sushi is ideal for a party; the ingredients are entirely up to your discretion. Generally, I place a variety of fish and vegetables on the center of the table and let people choose their own.

TEMARI SUSHI

MAKES 5 TEMARI (BALL) SUSHI

This sushi style traces its roots to the samurai era; it was popular among *maiko* (geisha apprentices) in Kyoto in the eighteenth century. Maiko couldn't eat big pieces of sushi; it made them look less elegant, and with these small balls with beautiful vegetables, there was not a strong fish smell. Temari sushi became a popular item to give to ladies. Its aesthetics represent the delightful and healthy Kyoto. When you visit Kyoto, make sure to stop by the kiosks at the train station. They sell lunch boxes with temari sushi, which has become a typical local art sushi.

---

5 oz (140 g) Sushi Rice (page 20)

2 slices tuna (see page 106 for cutting technique.)

2 slices salmon (see page 106 for cutting technique)

2 slices yellowtail or other white fish (see page 106 for cutting technique)

2 slices avocado, plus more for garnish (optional; see page 52 for cutting technique)

1 (2" [5-cm]) square piece kinshi tamago (egg sheet), julienned (see note)

Sliced jalapeño pepper (optional)

1 tbsp (15 g) orange tobiko (flying fish eggs; optional)

1 tbsp (15 g) green tobiko (optional)

1. Prepare five pieces of plastic wrap that are each about an 8-inch (20-cm) square. Moisten your hands with temizu (page 44) and form the rice into five 1-ounce (28-g) balls. Place one square of the plastic wrap on a cutting board and lay the tuna pieces, side by side, in the center of the square. Place one rice ball on the center of the fish. Gather the corners of the plastic wrap and tighten them to form a ball.

2. Using the remaining pieces of plastic wrap, repeat to make three more temari; one with the salmon, one with the yellowtail and one with the avocado. For the fifth ball, with the *kinshi tomago*, you can place a round of jalapeño on the plastic wrap first, if desired. If you want to further garnish your temari use tobiko. Before you unwrap the balls, make a small indentation on the top of each ball. Then, unwrap the balls and place the tobiko in the indentation. In my setup, I paired orange tobiko with the avocado temari and green tobiko with the yellowtail temari. If desired, you can add an extra slice of avocado to the salmon temari and a slice of jalapeño to the tuna temari.

*See beauty image on page 2.

CHEF ANDY'S NOTE: *Kinshi tamago* is very easy to make. In a medium-sized skillet over medium heat, heat 1½ teaspoons (7 ml) of vegetable oil. Beat one large egg and pour into the skillet. You should make a very thin egg sheet that looks almost like a crêpe. Remove from the heat once cooked through and julienne it into very thin strips, about 1/16 inch (2 mm) wide.

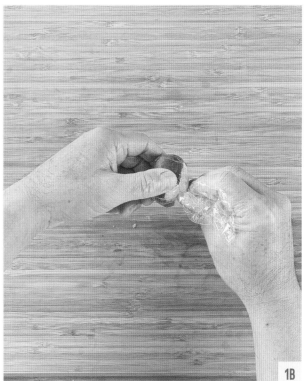

CHIRASHI SUSHI (SCATTERED SUSHI)

MAKES 1 BOWL

This style is very popular around March 3, when we celebrate Hinamatsuri (Girls' Day) in Japan. Parents created this dish by mixing sushi rice with many different cooked items from the ocean, such as shrimp, or the mountains, and even people's gardens, like shiitake or beans. The dish would have beautiful decorations and its purpose was to wish that your offspring kept growing healthy. The family would eat together and appreciate Mother Nature for her gifts. *Kaisen chirashi* has become very popular nowadays. It is a variation of this dish, whereby different kinds of seafood are placed and decorated on top of the rice. This sushi was served in a bowl because of a regulation of the eighteenth century of one bowl, one soup. This is a great one-bowl meal that is easily made at home. It could also be served in a martini glass or an avocado shell to make an attractive presentation. The term *chirashi* means "scattered," but you will notice that the items are layered to look scattered. This recipe can be made with almost any ingredients, so consider this recipe a guide rather than one that should be strictly followed.

---

5 oz (140 g) Sushi Rice (page 20)

2 tbsp (30 ml) sushi sauce (see page 15)

1 oz (28 g) kinshi tamago (egg sheet; see note for Temari Sushi, page 134), julienned

¼ (7½ x 8" [19 x 20–cm]) nori sheet, julienned thinly (you can cut with scissors—it will be easier!)

1 oz (28 g) daikon, julienned finely (see page 148 for cutting technique)

1 shiso leaf

1 sushi shrimp (see page 27 for prep technique)

1 oz (28 g) tuna, sliced (see page 106 for performing the Sogigiri Neta Cut)

1 oz (28 g) salmon, sliced (see page 106 for performing the Sogigiri Neta Cut)

1 oz (28 g) yellowtail, sliced (see page 106 for performing the Sogigiri Neta Cut)

5 pieces cucumber, sliced paper thin and cut in half, plus more for garnish

1 tsp wasabi paste

1 tsp pickled sushi ginger

10 thin slices red radish

1 small bunch kaiware (daikon sprouts), for garnish

1. Place the Sushi Rice in a bowl, pressing it down to create a flat surface. Drizzle the sushi sauce over the rice. Place the julienned kinshi tamago over the rice. Sprinkle some julienned nori over the egg. Place the julienned daikon at the back of the bowl, and the shiso leaf in front of the daikon. Place the sushi shrimp on the shiso leaf, tail pointing up. Now, we add the tuna, salmon and yellowtail, working our way to the front of the bowl. The cucumber slices can be fanned out and placed between the fish. Place the wasabi and pickled sushi ginger in the front of the bowl. Add the radish slices to the bowl. For further decoration you can also lay five of the red radish slices on a cutting board in a vertical line with the edges overlapping. Starting at the end closest to you, roll up the radish slices. Stand the roll up and press down on the top to create a "flower." Repeat with the remaining five radish slices, to make a second "flower." Garnish the bowl with more cucumber, radish flowers and daikon sprouts.

SASHIMI

Sashimi is the most high-end Japanese dish and is the oldest form of sushi, with some people saying the tradition goes back over 1,000 years, as originally eaten by fisherman. Serving sashimi in Japan started about 600 years ago. Sashimi is served at the beginning of the meal and is fish in its purest form. It consists mainly of fish and seafood decoration made by a sushi chef. In Japan, fish is seasonal. Each season, the fish on sashimi plates changes. The colors of the plates and the garnishes also change according to the season. During the spring, tai (red snapper) is the most famous in Japan; there's a whole-fish decoration on the plate. During winter, blowfish, also known as *fugu* in Japanese, is served as a superthin sashimi slice. This sashimi dish is called *tessa* in Japanese; it is so special that you need a special knife for it and chefs need a special certification to prepare it.

I want to share some general tips and reminders for when you are cutting sashimi. One of the most important things when cutting fish is that your knife is very sharp. A dull knife will damage the cells of the fish and cause it to deteriorate in quality. Tender and meaty fish, such as tuna, should be cut into thicker slices, so they don't fall apart when you are cutting them. Fish with tougher flesh, such as red snapper and halibut, should be sliced thinner. When you are about to perform your cuts, don't apply too much pressure on either your fish or your knife because it can damage the meat of the fish, which is very delicate by nature. When handling your filets, try to support them with both of your hands so the meat doesn't break.

Your cuts must be on the same side and very consistent. You must be very careful; not all fish and all parts of the fish can be served in sashimi. Sashimi must be taken from filets that are sushi grade, which means they are fresh and can be eaten raw. You can learn more on how to buy your fish and filets on page 26.

Sashimi decoration is very extensive and we will cover a couple of examples in this book. You can use many vegetables such as daikon or cucumber, and shiso leaf and many other leaves as well as flowers. Remember that you want to show the seasons in your sashimi plating, and you should use whatever items are in season locally. Sashimi is all about elegance and beauty. This is an art form, and it takes many years of experience and knowledge for sushi chefs to execute it properly. Throughout this chapter, I will run you through the basic sashimi decorating and cutting techniques that are used for most fish.

It took me about 6 months to feel comfortable with my garnishing skills. It requires a lot of patience and practice. Despite it being challenging, I had a very fun time working on it. For me, it is a great opportunity to be creative and artistic. It is always interesting to find a way to make an impressive decoration with the right use of color, balance, location on the plate, spacing and usage of garnish.

There are about only five or six sashimi-cutting techniques. Sashimi cutting and plating are simple, but they can make a strong impression on the plate. In this chapter you will learn some techniques for cutting sashimi, as well as decoration tips. When decorating sashimi plates, you use the principle *tenchijin*, which is a concept that comes from *ikebana*, a traditional flower-arranging technique. In ikebana, you take elements from nature to make the flower arrangements. The seasons are very important in this technique as well and must be reflected through them. In this chapter, you will learn more about how tenchijin translates into sashimi plating.

Let's get to it!

CUTTING FISH FOR SASHIMI:

THE HIKIGIRI CUT

The Hikigiri Cut is a "pulling cut" primarily used for tuna, salmon and yellowtail. You can use this cut in pretty much any fish that is tender. In this example, we will be using salmon to learn this technique. One thing to take into account before performing the Hikigiri Cut is that there will be a difference in the shape of your final pieces, depending on your fish and what kind of filet you are using. This happens mostly because all fish are different. Tuna filets, for one instance, tend to be in more "standardized" sizes because they come from way bigger loins, so the filets are cut in a rectangular shape. Salmon, on the other hand, has a smaller and longer body compared to tuna. Therefore, the loins have different shapes. This will create slightly different sizes in the final sashimi slices, which is normal and a part of this cut and cuisine. You will notice in this recipe that the salmon takes on a slightly triangular shape. Usually, when Hikigiri Cut pieces come from the tail (which is a thinner filet), the pieces may look triangular. When performing the Hikigiri Cut, we are aiming for bite-sized pieces, not focusing so much on the shape. Keep in mind the consistency of the pieces per fish. You want a piece that is ½ ounce (15 g).

---

1 salmon filet

1 shiso leaf

1 handful daikon, julienned (see page 148 for cutting technique)

Wasabi paste, for serving

Pickled sushi ginger, for serving

1. To perform a Hikigiri Cut, place the fish horizontally on a cutting board.

2. Determine the width of your slice, usually $3/8$ inch (1 cm).

3. Starting with the heel of the knife, draw your knife through the fish from heel to tip in one smooth stroke.

4. Repeat until you have an odd number of slices.

5. For simple plating for your sashimi, follow the instructions for Tenmori decoration (page 151).

2

3A

3B

CUTTING FISH FOR SASHIMI:

THE SOGIGIRI NETA CUT

The Sogigiri Neta Cut is a thinly sliced cut used on all kinds of fish. Particularly used to cut fish for nigiri, it can also be used for sashimi. In this example, we will be using yellowtail. It's ideal to start with a block of fish about as wide as the palm of your hand. Since you can use this cut for all types of fish, the thickness of your slices will be determined by the kind of fish you are cutting. White fish should be cut slightly thinner due to its flesh's chewy nature. For all the other fish, we will use the thickness stated in the following directions. Let's get to it!

1 yellowtail filet

1 shiso leaf

1 handful daikon, julienned (see page 148 for cutting technique)

Wasabi paste, for serving

Pickled sushi ginger, for serving

1. Place your filet at a 45-degree angle on a cutting board and slice a triangular portion from the end of the filet closest to you (you can save this piece to use for rolls). This will give you an angled surface.

2. Now, we will position the edge of the knife (the heel) on the fish and follow the angle we just created to slice a piece of fish that is 1 inch (2.5 cm) wide, 2 inches (5 cm) long and ¼ inch (6 mm) thick.

3. Repeat until you have an odd number of slices.

4. For a beautiful plating idea, follow the Hanamori technique for decoration (page 152).

CUTTING FISH FOR SASHIMI:

THE KAKUGIRI CUT

The Kakugiri Cut is a dice cut that is used primarily for tuna and salmon, but it can also be used with other fish. It's a popular cut when making poke (see page 83). In this example, we will be using tuna to learn this technique.

---

1 block-cut tuna filet

1 shiso leaf

1 handful daikon, julienned (see page 148 for cutting technique)

Wasabi paste, for serving

Pickled sushi ginger, for serving

1. Slice your fish on a cutting board, using the Hikigiri Cut (see page 140).

2. Place your slices flat and vertically on the cutting board.

3. Cut them into cubes by using the whole blade of your knife. The size of the cubes depends on what you are using the fish for. If you are serving them as sashimi, they will sometimes have a more rectangular shape, but your cubes should be ½ inch (1.3 mm) wide by ½ inch (1.3 mm) long. True cubes of about ¼ inch (6 mm) on every side are commonly used for poke. I leave it to your creativity.

4. For simple plating of your Kakugiri Cuts, follow instructions for Tenmori decoration (page 151).

CUTTING FISH FOR SASHIMI:

THE USUZUKURI CUT

This is a technique in which fish is sliced superthin. The Usuzukuri Cut is primarily used on white fish due to the rigidity of the meat for some of these fish. Your goal is to have a slice that is so thin that you can see through it. I like to serve it with yakumi (see page 126) and Ponzu (page 160), a perfect pairing. In this example we will be using halibut to learn this technique.

---

1 halibut filet

1 shiso leaf

1 handful daikon, julienned (see page 148 for cutting technique)

Wasabi paste, for serving

Pickled sushi ginger, for serving

1. Place the filet at a 45-degree angle on a cutting board. Slice a triangular portion off the end of the filet closest to you. This will give you an angled surface.

2. Position your knife nearly flat so that your final slice is 1 inch (2.5 cm) wide and 2 inches (5 cm) long, and as thin as possible.

3. Place the fingertips of your left hand on the fish to support and steady it. Start the cut with the heel of your knife and draw the knife toward you through the fish, using the whole blade. Remember that this cut is paper thin, so that the final slice is almost transparent.

4. Finish cutting the slice with the tip of the knife in a vertical position.

5. Carefully pick up the fish with your left hand and place it directly on your serving plate. You want to place your slices slightly overlapping each other in a semi-circle, leaving the center for your garnish.

6. If you have the engawa part of halibut (see page 126), place your engawa strip horizontally on your cutting board and make vertical cuts of about ¼ inch (6 mm) wide throughout the whole strip.

7. Place your engawa pieces in front of your garnish, by following instructions for Tenmori decoration (see page 151). Add wasabi and pickled sushi ginger to the plate.

CUTTING FISH FOR SASHIMI:

THE BUTTERFLY CUT

To serve scallops for sashimi, you must at least cut them in half, so they are bite-sized. To add flair to your scallop sashimi, you can use this technique. Also, when you butterfly a scallop, you will be able to make nigiri with it. To make scallop nigiri, perform the Butterfly Cut as explained here and then assemble your nigiri following the instructions on page 108. Usually, scallops are sold frozen. You want to defrost them slowly by leaving them in your fridge overnight on absorbent paper towels. Then, the scallops are pretty much ready to go. After defrosting them the first time, you can put them back in your fridge for up to 2 days. When storing them in your fridge, plastic wrap them.

3 scallops

1 shiso leaf

1 handful daikon, julienned (see page 148 for cutting technique)

3 half-lemon slices (cut a lemon in half lengthwise and then slice thinly)

Wasabi paste, for serving

Pickled sushi ginger, for serving

1. To perform your Butterfly Cut, place each scallop on a cutting board and slice it in half, stopping about ¼ inch (6 mm) from the edge.

2. Open the scallop with the cut side down.

3. You can plate your scallops by placing a base of daikon and a shiso leaf on a small plate. Interlace an odd number of scallops and half-lemon slices and place them on top of the shiso leaf. Add some wasabi and pickled sushi ginger to the plate.

NOTES ON GARNISHING SASHIMI:

HOW TO CUT DAIKON

Daikon, the white radish, is used as a base for sashimi plates. It is also used in Chirashi Sushi (page 136) and is generally just good for you. Daikon is high in fiber and low in carbohydrates, and is said to aid in digestion. Milder than red radish, it adds a pleasing crunch to salads. You can also incorporate it into soups and stir-fried dishes.

Daikon cut into a fine julienne is called *tsuma*, which is also a broader term for "garnish." Cutting the daikon in this fashion is the main garnish for sashimi. Sushi chefs need to make a lot of tsuma, so they use a mandoline to do this. However, when they cut it themselves, they use the Katsuramuki technique. Julienning daikon is a great practice for knife control, a very important skill for sushi chefs. The Katsuramuki technique is not only used by professional chefs; most Japanese home cooks actually manage to master the technique because it is widely used in Japanese cuisine.

Some care must be taken performing the Katsuramuki technique. It requires practice, so we will start with one piece of a quartered daikon with the ultimate goal being to cut 3-inch (7.5-cm)-long pieces. To make your garnish curly, place your stack vertically on your cutting board. This is called *yoko ken*. To make your garnish straight, place your stack horizontally on your cutting board. This is called *tate ken*.

These directions have been written with a right-handed person in mind; if you are left-handed, simply mirror the instructions.

1. Slice a 3-inch (7.5-cm) piece of a quartered daikon. Holding the daikon piece in your left hand and the knife in your right hand, insert the knife under the skin and remove the skin, slicing carefully around the outside of the daikon, until you reach the clean white flesh inside.

2. Gently push the daikon under the knife while moving the knife up and down. The only movement the knife should make is a slight up-and-down motion.

3. As you are turning the daikon, you will make a long strip. Cut the strip into equal lengths and create a stack. Slice your stack into paper-thin strands.

4. Place in a bowl with water and set aside until you are ready to use.

CHEF ANDY'S NOTE: This technique can also be used for cucumbers. When using tsuma for sashimi decoration, we grab a handful of it. It is not common to measure the amount. You want to have enough to create a little height for your shiso leaf or cucumber to rest upon.

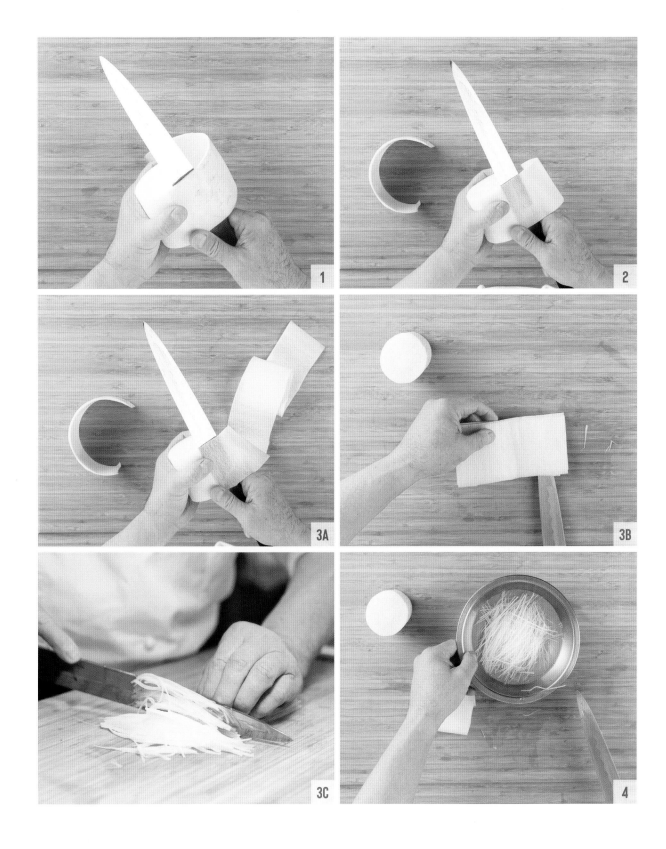

NOTES ON SASHIMI DECORATION

TENMORI

The Tenmori (center-high) decoration technique is used for simple plating and decoration. As with most dishes in Japanese cuisine, we must pay special attention to sashimi decoration since fish and seafood are expensive and we must respect its value through our careful plating. This plating technique is mostly used when plating a sashimi serving with a single kind of fish.

1. To execute Tenmori, place a handful of julienned daikon (see page 148 for cutting technique) in a mountain on the center of your plate.

2. In front or at the base of that little white mountain, place a shiso leaf. If you don't have shiso leaves, use thinly cut cucumber slices.

3. Now, take your fish slices and make a fan with them. Place them in front of the shiso leaf.

4. Serve with some pickled sushi ginger and wasabi.

NOTES ON SASHIMI PLATING:

HANAMORI

The Hanamori technique will make a beautiful flower out of your fish slices. This adds a special flair to your sashimi plates and will definitely impress your guests. You can use this decoration technique with any kind of fish. In this example we will be using yellowtail to learn this technique.

2½ oz (75 g) yellowtail (see below for how to slice)

1 shiso leaf

1 handful daikon, julienned (see page 148 for daikon cutting technique)

Wasabi paste, for serving

Pickled sushi ginger, for serving

1. Make five ½-ounce (15-g) slices of yellowtail, using the Sogigiri Neta Cut (see page 106).

2. As you cut your slices, line them up vertically on the cutting board overlapping the edges by ½ inch (1.3 cm). Start from top to bottom when placing your slices on the cutting board.

3. Starting from bottom to top and using your fingers, roll up the line of fish and then stand it up.

4. You can use your fingers or chopsticks to shape the flower. This can be part of a sashimi combination plate or served on its own. Plate on top of a shiso leaf and diakon, and add wasabi and pickled sushi ginger to the plate.

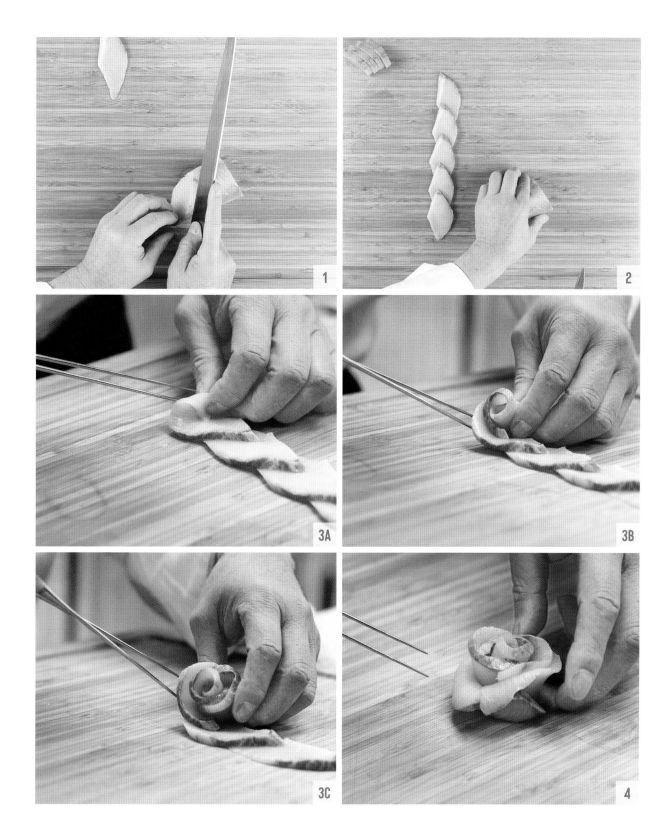

CHEF ANDY'S SASHIMI PLATE

Sashimi plates are often served with a variety of garnishes, called tsuma, which, while decorative, are meant to cleanse the palate between different types of fish. *Moritsuke* (sashimi plate decoration) is composed of three parts: *ten* (sky), *chi* (ground) and *jin* (human). This form of decoration comes from Mother Nature.

Ten and chi always have the same relationship on the plate, but the jin is mobile. The other key to sashimi decoration is the relationship of space: 40 percent of the plate is for sashimi while the other 60 percent is empty. Daikon radish cut into tsuma using the Katsuramuki technique is an important garnish when making sashimi; see page 148. Fish should be cut into pieces that are bite-sized and easy to pick up with chopsticks. Each type of fish should be the same size. Traditionally, sashimi is served in an odd number of slices.

Color is also a key element to Japanese cuisine. There are five traditional Japanese colors that are used in plating, which are black, white, red, yellow and green. We try to include each color in all of our dishes through the ingredients or the sauces. To build a sample combination sashimi plate, we will need the following ingredients. Don't worry if you don't have everything. Feel free to substitute.

Wasabi paste

3 slices octopus (see page 30 for prep technique; see below for cutting technique)

2 handfuls shredded daikon (see page 148 for cutting technique)

1 shiso leaf

3 slices tuna (cut using the Hikigiri Cut; see page 140)

3 slices salmon (cut using the Sogigiri Neta Cut; see page 142)

3 slices halibut (cut using the Usuzukuri Cut; see page 145)

4 thin cucumber slices (see page 51 for cutting technique), cut in half

Red radish, sliced thinly and cut in half (optional)

1. First, we will make a wasabi leaf for decoration. Take a small ball of wasabi and place it on a cutting board. Press down and form into the shape of a leaf. Rotate the wasabi so that the top of the leaf is pointing toward you. Using your knife, press a line down the middle. Using the tip of your knife make lines on each side at a 45-degree angle to create the veins of the leaf. Set aside (see photo on page 137).

2. Next, we will cut our octopus slices, using the Namigiri Cut. After you have prepped your octopus, remove one tentacle. Take your tentacle and, starting at the widest part of it, hold your knife, starting at the heel, and pull the knife toward you, making a "wave" cut by changing the angle of your knife every ¼ inch (6 mm) as you draw it toward you—do this by lifting the knife and then going down flat. You can hit the slice with the heel of your knife to tenderize it even more. Place your octopus slices aside as you assemble the plate.

3. Select a round plate. Begin by placing the daikon on the plate and pulling it up into the shape of a mountain. Place the shiso leaf against the daikon. Stand the tuna slices up against the shiso leaf (this is the "ten"). The salmon is next, placed to the left of the tuna (this is the "chi"). The halibut will be placed right in front of the tuna. We have now created a triangular shape. Place the halibut close to the tuna, then two pieces of octopus on the right side of the halibut. (The halibut and octopus are the "jin.") The wasabi will be right in front. In between the fish, artistically place your sliced cucumber and radish (if using) to add balance to the color.

THE SAUCES

The three main sauces in Japan are soy sauce, nitsume (eel sauce, a.k.a. sushi sauce) and Ponzu (page 160). Most of the sauces that we see on sushi rolls have been created outside Japan. In Japan, we have vinegar "sauces," such as *amazu*, *nihaizu*, *sanbaizu* and ponzu. The reason Japan has so many vinegar sauces is that Japanese cooking is water-based, whereas the cuisines of many other countries is oil-based. In water-based cooking, you try to enhance or extract the natural flavors with water. Japanese cuisine utilizes a lot of boiling, simmering and steaming. These are all techniques that are water-based. The introduction of Buddhism in the sixth century denied the use of animal fats to Japanese people and that's how their water-based cuisine was born. Oil-based cuisines use more fat when cooking, making the flavors stronger, therefore the need for even stronger flavors to match them in their sauces. Soy sauce is very important in Japan because its roots come from Japanese Buddhism. In the old days, all ingredients used when cooking had to be vegetables. Soybeans were one of the proteins that came from the garden. Eventually, it became a popular sauce. Sauces from other countries tend to be spicy, sweet or salty or have a very strong taste.

I love to create my own sauces according to what I am serving, and I like to use seasonal ingredients every time. For Japanese chefs, the natural flavor of the ingredients is very important. That's why, even though Japanese chefs include foreign sauces in their recipes, they are always mild so the natural flavors of the ingredients can pop up more. Japanese-foreign sauces tend to be balanced and soft—just enough to complement the food, not overpower it.

It is popular to use sauces on top of special sushi rolls. It has become an important part of it. However, Japanese people are not very fond of sauces except when having foreign foods. Foreign sauces, such as ketchup and mayonnaise, have become very popular among Japanese people. I don't like when special rolls are covered in all kinds of sauces. I think it overpowers the roll and you can taste only the sauce. As I've explained before, I'm used to tasting the natural flavors of the ingredients and feeling the harmony among them. That's why I pair only traditional Japanese sauces with nigiri. The sauce is to complement the fish and make it stand out. Usually, we just brush a little sauce on top of the fish of the nigiri to enhance the harmony of the ingredients.

I use sauces as decoration most of the time when serving sushi rolls. I think it is interesting for beginners to play and get creative with sauces. It is a good first step. It is very important to consider to whom you are serving your food. You want your guests to enjoy your meal and there is no right or wrong in terms of using the sauces. There are times where Japanese sauces will be the best pairing and some other times where fusion sauces can be game changers. Just one note: Don't put Spicy Mayo (page 158) on nigiri if your guests are Japanese.

Color is a very important element to Japanese cuisine. Sometimes the five traditional colors of Japanese cuisine (black, white, red, yellow and green) are included on the plating with sauce and not only through the ingredients. Having all the colors is important for balance on our dishes. Some of the sauce recipes in this chapter can be used to represent these colors.

KANIKAMA SAUCE

MAKES 2 TABLESPOONS (30 ML)

For me, sauces should complement the natural flavors of the ingredients. The saltiness of the soy sauce and sweetness from the mirin along with the creamy texture of the mayonnaise complement the fishy sensation of the kanikama (imitation crab), giving an extra-nice flavor to the roll.

4 tsp (20 ml) mayonnaise

1 tsp mirin

1 tsp soy sauce

1. In a small bowl, stir together the mayonnaise, mirin and soy sauce, then set the mixture aside. You can prepare this ahead of time and place the bowl, covered in plastic wrap, in the refrigerator. You can keep this sauce in your fridge for a week. I recommend that you store it in a covered plastic container.

SPICY MAYO

MAKES ½ CUP (120 ML)

Spicy mayo is very popular here in Los Angeles, so I created my own version of this favorite. I think that the ingredients used here become a great pairing for any kind of fish and elevate the taste of special rolls; it also goes well with soy sauce. I like to use premade *toubanjan* (Chinese chili paste) for this recipe because it doesn't have a strong garlic flavor. Toubanjan can be found mostly in Asian markets and online.

I recommend mixing this sauce with your favorite diced pieces of fish left over from making other rolls. Not only is it a delicious meal, but it also helps reduce the amount of wasted food. Sometimes restaurants cannot use their leftovers for their main dishes, but in Japan, we try to use them by creating different recipes.

½ cup (120 g) mayonnaise

4 tsp (20 ml) toubanjan, plus more to taste

4 tsp (20 ml) sesame oil

1. Place the mayonnaise in a small bowl and gradually add the toubanjan until the sauce reaches your desired level of spiciness. Add the sesame oil and stir well. Cover with plastic wrap and refrigerate until needed. You can keep this sauce in your fridge for a week. I recommend that you store it in a covered plastic container.

WASABI MAYO (GREEN SAUCE)

MAKES ⅓ CUP (80 ML)

In Japanese plating, we use five colors; you can represent green with this recipe. We can create green from an array of ingredients, but I always try to use at least one Japanese ingredient in my recipes. Wasabi in this case, which also adds a very special taste. The perfect thickness of this sauce allows you to create easy designs on your plate. Mayonnaise, besides being liked by many people, has a great texture that makes it easier to mix with other ingredients or sauces.

1 tbsp (15 g) wasabi paste
¼ cup (60 ml) mayonnaise
1 tbsp (15 ml) honey

1. In a small bowl, combine the wasabi with the mayonnaise. Mix well and add the honey. Adjust the proportions according to your taste. You can keep this sauce in your fridge for a week. I recommend that you store it in a covered plastic container.

HONEY MUSTARD SAUCE
(YELLOW SAUCE)

MAKES ABOUT ½ CUP (120 ML)

This sauce produces another of the five colors for Japanese plating: yellow. Taking advantage of the versatility and popularity of mayonnaise, I add freshly made Japanese mustard paste to the mayonnaise and honey to balance the spiciness of the mustard. The result is this yellow-colored sauce that can elevate your dish.

2 tbsp (18 g) dry mustard
2 tbsp (30 ml) water
¼ cup (60 ml) mayonnaise
2 tbsp (30 ml) honey, plus more to taste

1. In a small bowl, mix the dry mustard with the water and set aside for a few minutes to allow the flavor to develop. Gradually add the mayonnaise to the mustard while mixing to develop a uniform color. Taste the sauce and add the honey until the sauce reaches your desired flavor. I personally like it slightly on the sweeter side, so I add more honey. You can keep this sauce in your fridge for a week. I recommend that you store it in a covered plastic container.

PONZU

MAKES 9 OZ (266 ML)

Ponzu is a citrus-based soy sauce. The reason for the citrus is to bring down the strong flavor of pure soy sauce. This light tangy sauce is the favorite for most nigiri and sashimi lovers. It is a great pairing for fish, especially white fish, such as halibut or snapper. It is also used for cooked dishes and falls into the category of a more traditional Japanese sauce.

¼ cup (60 ml) cup fresh lemon or lime juice

¼ cup (60 ml) soy sauce

¼ cup (60 ml) rice vinegar

¼ cup (60 ml) mirin

2 tbsp (30 ml) tamari

1 (3" [7.5-cm]) square piece konbu

1. In a jar with an airtight lid, combine the citrus juice, soy sauce, rice vinegar, mirin and tamari with the konbu. Allow the sauce to age in the refrigerator for 2 weeks before you use it. The konbu will mellow and enhance the sauce. This sauce can be stored indefinitely in your fridge, and I recommend that you store it in a covered plastic container. You don't need to remove the konbu from the sauce after the aging process.

CHEF ANDY'S NOTE: This sauce can also be used in many ways. As an example, ponzu sauce mixed with sesame oil and mustard paste is a good sauce for seared foods.

HONEY SRIRACHA (RED SAUCE)

MAKES ½ CUP (120 ML)

This is another of the five colors for Japanese plating: red. I use only two ingredients here—sriracha and honey. Honey adds a sweet layer to sriracha, which makes its spiciness more enjoyable. I use this sauce frequently in my plating to add contrasting color.

¼ cup (60 ml) honey
¼ cup (60 ml) sriracha

1. In a small bowl, combine the honey and sriracha. Taste and adjust the proportions to suit your taste. Store in a covered plastic container in the refrigerator for up to 3 months.

SRIRACHA MAYO (ORANGE SAUCE)

MAKES ABOUT 1/3 CUP (80 ML)

This is a variation on an orange sauce, great for the five colors of Japanese plating. It is different from my Spicy Mayo (page 158), but most restaurants use these ingredients when making their spicy mayo. Sriracha, which is used in this recipe, contains vinegar, which gives it a tangier flavor and overpowers the natural flavor of fish, whereas toubanjan, which I use for my Spicy Mayo, complements the natural flavor of the fish. Mayonnaise helps make the spiciness of sriracha more enjoyable and endurable for people not used to spicy sauces. My students love to use this sauce when they are plating their sushi rolls.

¼ cup (60 ml) mayonnaise
2 tbsp (30 ml) sriracha

1. In a small bowl, combine the mayonnaise and sriracha. Taste and adjust the proportions to suit your taste Store in a covered plastic container in the refrigerator for up to 3 months.

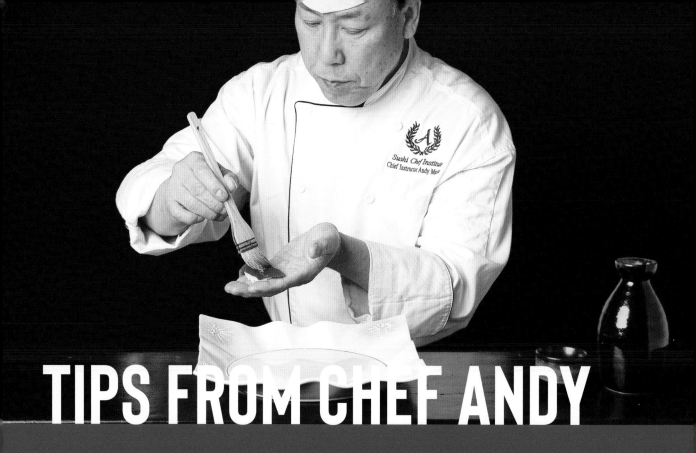

TIPS FROM CHEF ANDY

To close off our journey, I want to discuss how to properly eat sushi and enjoy your sushi bar experience. Sushi has been welcomed in many parts of the world and I want to give you some more insight on our culture and the manners expected at the sushi bar, which not many people have the opportunity to learn. I want to share these tips with you, and impart you with the mission of sharing it with your friends and loved ones, so we continue to spread the joy of Japanese food culture.

Many Japanese sushi chefs always say, "Learn by eye." Not many are willing to teach step by step, and thus, unfortunately many skills and techniques remain unshared and lost. Some principles and ideas might be natural for us Japanese people because they are part of our culture, but that does not hold true for foreigners.

I like to share everything I know with the next generation of chefs and sushi lovers. A big part of my knowledge is not my own; it is experience and knowledge passed on to me by elder chefs. I feel that now I have the duty of passing it on to next generation. I want my students to do the same and pass it on to the next person and keep Japanese food culture alive around the world. Knowledge can create great relationships with people from different walks of life.

The knowledge and experience that I've gained throughout my life has helped me during all my years. I want it to do the same for you. I hope that you keep learning more Japanese fundamental skills and culture. We need to keep going in that direction, understanding and learning about other cultures so we have a peaceful, healthy and safer world. I hope I get to see you in my classroom someday!

THE PROPER WAY TO EAT SUSHI

Let the fish side fall to the left and rice side to the right. Pick up the nigiri with your thumb and index finger, then dip into soy sauce on the fish side. Don't use too much sauce; it will overpower the taste of the fish and rice. Bring the sushi to your mouth with the fish side toward your tongue. You should taste the soy sauce and fish with the wasabi flavor and then finally the sushi rice in your mouth. Eventually, it will become a mixture of all the flavors in your mouth.

Nigiri sushi is a different experience each time, it is always a different flavor from the fish and sauces. You should go from mild fish to oily fish, then marinated fish and finish with sweet egg sushi or eel with sweet sauce. You can always eat pickled sushi ginger in between to cleanse your palate and to better enjoy the natural flavor of the fish.

HOW TO ENJOY THE SUSHI BAR

Usually, sushi bars can seat about 10 guests. The guests face the sushi chef to be able to see the chef work. Please be aware that the sushi chefs at the sushi bar need to take care of each guest, so be patient. The sushi bar is to enjoy and relax and take your time enjoying the dishes you order or that your chef has prepared for you. Strong perfumes are prohibited at the sushi bar. These intervene with one of the sushi bar principles for a true sushi bar experience, *gokan*, which is related to the nuances of our senses, and a fundamental part of the sushi bar experience. You should be able to smell, see, touch, hear and taste while in the sushi bar.

If it is your first time at a sushi bar, don't do omakase (chef's choice) right away. The best way to enjoy omakase is when you create a relationship with your chef and your chef understands your taste. Communicate with the chefs with a big voice. It is hard for them to hear you from the other side of the bar. Ask questions about your food, ask for recommendations but remember you might not be the only one wanting to interact with the chef, so be aware of your surroundings and other guests so your sushi chef can provide the best service to everyone. Sushi chefs enjoy communication and a happy smile. They want you to have the best time. Say "thank you" to your chef; sushi chefs will remember you and a good relationship will start. From that point, every time you come back to the sushi bar, you will have a great experience. The more you ask questions and learn at the sushi bar, the more you will enjoy your food. Appreciate the art of decoration, garnish and the creativity of the chef as they affect your plate.

You can use your fingers to pick up and eat the sushi at the sushi bar. Do not dip your sushi into too much soy sauce. In omakase style, your chef has already put sauce on your fish, so try it as it is served before adding anything else. Sushi chefs usually prepare a balanced flavor for you to enjoy. You can request wasabi and sauces from the chef. You can ask them to modify the amount that is served to you. The same applies to sushi rice.

If you are seated at a table, you can use chopsticks. At a sushi bar, when in front of the chef, I prefer to use my fingers, but chopsticks can be used as well. In Japan, we have manners on how to use chopsticks. One of these rules is to not poke your food with the chopsticks. Another is to not pass food among diners from chopsticks to chopsticks. Eat slowly and cleanly; this is a more formal way to eat. Your sushi chef will appreciate you upgrading your sushi bar manners and you will also have a more enjoyable experience by understanding the culture of Japan as well.

Irashaimase Japan. Welcome to Japan.

ACKNOWLEDGMENTS

I want to thank Edward Klevens, Miguel Hurtado (MiruDaru), Setsu Matsuda, Franny Donington-Ayad and the team of Page Street Publishing for their effort in helping me put together and share this piece of my knowledge and culture with the world.

ABOUT THE AUTHOR

Chef Andy Matsuda was born near Kobe, Japan, in 1956. When he was nine years old, his family started a small Japanese restaurant where he learned the joy of cooking. After graduating from high school, he began to work as an apprentice at Genpachi, one of the most famous restaurants in Osaka; he worked there for five years. He also became a member of a sushi chef organization called Yosei-kai. At the age of 23, he returned to his hometown to help expand the family business. A couple of years later, at the age of 25, his new challenge in life was to move to Los Angeles, California.

His first job was in Little Tokyo, as a kitchen assistant, but within a week, he was promoted to chief sushi chef. Since then, Chef Matsuda has worked at fine sushi bars in Santa Monica, Aspen, New York and has had the opportunity to work for major hotels where he learned other ethnic cuisines such as French, Italian and Thai, among others.

At the age of 36, Chef Matsuda faced the biggest challenge of his life; he was diagnosed with colon cancer and began the battle for his life. Going through four years of intensive treatments and self-reflection, he began to understand the relationship between food and health, people and environment. Overcoming cancer, he was full of appreciation and wanted to somehow pay back his debt of gratitude to American society. This is his gift to America.

In 2002, he started a sushi chef training school in downtown Los Angeles, called the Sushi Chef Institute, now located in Torrance, California. He's taught beginners and professional chefs from all over the world since then.

"As a chef, I would like to impart my knowledge of sushi to various people, in an accurate and comprehensive manner, for them to discover new aspects of sushi and gain more interests in this field. I would like to teach and pass on my way of gratitude toward nature, love among individuals and peace among countries. I hope to instill the core of my teaching philosophy, which is based on my profound appreciation for nature, family and society, to people from all walks of life."

INDEX